GW00640695

LITTLE BOXES

Two Plays

by

JOHN BOWEN

SAMUEL FRENCH

LONDON
NEW YORK TORONTO SYDNEY HOLLYWOOD

348600

LITTLE BOXES

First presented at the Hampstead Theatre Club on the 26th February 1968; subsequently at the Duchess Theatre, London, with the following cast of characters:

(in order of their appearance)

THE COFFEE LACE

ROSE	*Sylvia Coleridge*
IRIS	*Maureen Pryor*
LILY	*June Jago*
MR DAVIS	*David Cook*
SONNY	*Frank Middlemass*
JIMMY	*Larry Noble*
JOHNNY	*Peter Howell*
MADGE	*Angela Thorne*
MISS PEEL	*Anna Cropper*

TREVOR

JANE KEMPTON	*Anna Cropper*
SARAH LAWRENCE	*Angela Thorne*
TREVOR	*David Cook*
MRS LAWRENCE	*June Jago*
MR LAWRENCE	*Frank Middlemass*
MRS KEMPTON	*Maureen Pryor*
MR KEMPTON	*Peter Howell*
MR HUDSON	*Larry Noble*

The plays directed by PHILIP GROUT
Settings by J. HUTCHINSON SCOTT

The action of the plays passes in two identically shaped flats, the first in Kennington, the second in Kensington

Time—the present

AUTHOR'S NOTES

THESE plays are designed as a double bill. They are both plays about people who live in boxes. In the first play, the people are old, and they get out. In the second, they are young, and are shut in.

The set for both plays should be identical in shape, but differently dressed in each case, since the people of the first play are poor and live in Kennington, and those of the second are rich and live in Kensington. The same actors should play in each play. Unfortunately there is one more character in the first play than in the second. If I had been cleverer, there would have been the same number in each.

THE COFFEE LACE

SCENE I

SCENE—*The top-floor flat of a decayed Victorian house in Kennington. A day in February.*

There are three rooms and a lavatory. The smallest of the three rooms is at a higher level than the others, and is reached by a short staircase, opening off a passage that runs the full length of the stage and divides the largest room (L) *from the others. This is the room belonging to* LILY *and* JOHNNY, *and it has a kitchen alcove screened off at the back.* SONNY *and* IRIS *live on the same level, their door opening directly opposite that of Lily's room, separated only by the passage.* ROSE *and* JIMMY *live in the small room upstairs. Only the lavatory door is seen, at the upstage end of the passage. Next to it, but opening* R *off the passage, is the door to the downstairs world. Each room has a double bed, but the two smaller rooms are otherwise sparsely furnished. Lily and Johnny's room is also the common room for the three couples. It is the only one with a gas-fire in it. Each of the others has a small, round portable electric fire, giving little heat. The rooms, the clothes and the furniture are worn and shabby. What photographs and bric-a-brac there are give evidence of a theatrical past before the 1939–45 war.*

When the CURTAIN *rises,* ROSE *and* JIMMY *are discovered sitting on the edge of their bed, crouched over the fire.* ROSE *wears an eiderdown over day clothes,* JIMMY *a blanket, and both wear woolly gloves.* IRIS *is sitting on the bed in her room reading the "Reader's Digest".* SONNY *is sitting on the piano stool* R. *Both wear overcoats.* SONNY *is stitching sequins on to a blouse.* LILY *is in bed in her room, giving a lesson to* MR DAVIS, *the young man from the pawnshop, who is sitting on the stool* R *of the bed balancing a book on his head—it is a deportment lesson. He wears an overcoat.* MR DAVIS *wishes to become an actor, but has been persuaded that he needs coaching before applying to one of the acting schools for an audition. All the occupants of the flat are in their sixties, but he is from the world outside. Unless indicated, the characters in those rooms where the action is not, for the time being, concentrated, simply sit still.*

ROSE. It's cold here, very cold. We've got the draughty room, we've always had it.

IRIS. You get no heat from one bar. You might as well have it off.

LILY. When ugly people fall in love, it is never with other ugly people. One might think it more suitable if they did, but they do not.

MR DAVIS. Yes, Miss Terralozzi.

LILY. Luckily beautiful people seldom fall in love with anyone at all, so they may as well marry ugly people as not. That is why I married Mr Sims.

MR DAVIS. The vicar had a word with me.

LILY. You have a gap in your teeth, Mr Davis.

MR DAVIS. He was wondering . . .

LILY. A gap. A distinct gap.

MR DAVIS. He wondered if you'd consent to appear at the Senior Citizens' Evening. In a professional capacity. There'd be Old Time Dancing after, but you'd not be expected to join in.

LILY. We never go out. You know that.

MR DAVIS. There'd be a fee. Two guineas the vicar said. There's a special fund to cover it in Church Expenses. The Senior Citizens' Entertainment Fund.

LILY. Two guineas?

MR DAVIS. Yes.

LILY. Eight and sixpence each. Please inform the vicar that artistes of our standing do not appear for eight and sixpence. Meanwhile, you have a gap in your teeth. You must have it filled. I spoke of this at our last lesson.

MR DAVIS. You always speak of it.

LILY. For an artist, a good appearance is half the battle. More than half. I've known people in the profession who had nothing else.

MR DAVIS (*rising*) I went to the dentist. (*He moves down* L, *balancing the book*)

LILY. Excellent.

MR DAVIS. He said it'd cost me.

LILY. What?

MR DAVIS (*moving down* R) Money, Miss Terralozzi.

LILY. Is there no National Health?

MR DAVIS. Not for cosmetics. He said if it's not for chewing, it's cosmetic.

LILY. Then you must use the teeth that come into your pawnshop.

MR DAVIS. They wouldn't fit me. You have to have them fitted. Anyway nobody pawns teeth nowadays. (*He moves down* L)

LILY. Nonsense. It's well known that the poor pawn their teeth. (*Calling*) Iris!

(ROSE *and* JIMMY *look at each other. So do* SONNY *and* IRIS)

SONNY. She wants you.

IRIS. Showing off. She wants to show off. She wants to show she can call me, and I come.

LILY (*calls*) Iris, dear!

(IRIS *gets up, takes off her overcoat, then crosses the hall to Lily's room, and enters*)

Iris, do the poor pawn their teeth?

IRIS. Is that why you called?

LILY. Mr Davis was asking. He has an interest.

IRIS. I've known it done. I've heard of it.

LILY (*to Mr Davis*) Miss Fellowes comes of a very poor home. She knows these things.

MR DAVIS. Yes, Miss Terralozzi.

LILY. In Miss Fellowes's day, many of us in the profession were born into poverty. It was no disgrace, you understand. Miss Fellowes raised herself.

IRIS. If you've finished the lesson, we'll come in by the fire where it's warm.

LILY. You have your own fire.

IRIS. It's getting dark in there. Grey. You can't have the fire and the light both on, you know that.

LILY (*looking at Mr Davis*) Please, Iris, dear. Please. (*To Mr Davis*) What is the time, Mr Davis?

MR DAVIS. I've only had forty-five minutes.

LILY. I shall not cheat you. (*To Iris*) In fifteen minutes, Miss Fellowes.

IRIS. I could stay and hear him with you. (*To Mr Davis*) You'd benefit from an audience.

(MR DAVIS *is alarmed*)

LILY. I shall decide when Mr Davis is ready to expose himself to the public, Miss Fellowes. (*Indicating the door*) If you please.

(IRIS *hesitates, and goes out. She slams the door.* ROSE *hears it, and looks at* JIMMY. *He gets up, goes down the stairs from their room, and is in time to see* IRIS *going into hers.* IRIS *sits down.* JIMMY *returns to* ROSE)

LILY (*meanwhile*) Please continue, Mr Davis.

(MR DAVIS *takes the book from his head, moves* R *to the door and begins to read, in mime*)

IRIS (*entering her room*) She's got that fire going full blast. (*Putting on her coat*) She doesn't need it. She's in bed. She has the body warmth. (*She sits on the bed*)

SONNY. The boy needs it.

IRIS. He has his overcoat. He can wear that. Five shillings an hour! Anyone else would charge a pound.

SONNY. We have to keep him sweet, dear. We have to keep that boy sweet. He gave us three pound on your cameo brooch. I don't know how he explains it to Mr Simon.

IRIS. It was worth six.

SONNY. No, dear, not that brooch. Not six.

IRIS. I wore that brooch all through *The Dollar Princess*. I wore it in the Garden Party scene in Act Two.

SONNY. Just the same, dear, you know as well as I do, you picked it up for half a crown at a totter's in Greenwich.

(*The action returns to the main room*)

LILY. For a while, we had an act of our own, you know. The

Three Posies, with Sonny and Jim. My husband managed it.

Iris. We should go in. Ridiculous. Wasting the fire.

Mr Davis. I never see your husband.

Iris. He learns nothing.

Lily. You see him in the shop.

Mr Davis. Yes, he comes to the shop sometimes. But, I mean, he's not here, is he? I don't meet him.

Lily. Mr Sims goes out a great deal. His work takes him to the City.

Mr Davis. Ah . . .

Lily. Mr Sims deals with the business side of things.

Mr Davis. That's right. I give him three pound on a cameo brooch.

Lily. In the profession, Mr Davis, we are not expected to know about the business side. Mr Sims had money of his own when I married him. He had a private income. Miss Fellowes and Miss Deveraux married within the profession, but that was not at all usual. It shows a lack of self-respect. In Miss Deveraux, I could understand it. She was never serious. We are all very fond of Miss Deveraux here, but she has been a frivolous little thing all her life, and it does no good to deny it. She might have married a specialist in Nervous Diseases at the Charing Cross Hospital, but as one might expect, she gave too much too soon.

Mr Davis. I'm nervous myself, Miss Terralozzi. I've always been nervous, as a matter of fact. That's why I want to go on the stage.

Lily. Mr Sims used to come to *Dancing with Daisy* at least three times a week. He booked a stall for the run, always the same stall. And when *I* appeared, he would burst into spontaneous applause.

Iris. She's never been a true professional. We should take it in turns, teaching him. Then we'd have the fire.

Mr Davis (*uncertainly*) I had a letter from my mother . . .

Lily. Yes?

Mr Davis. She was listening to Women's Hour on the wireless. There was this lady talking about dramatic movement.

Lily. What *about* dramatic movement?

Mr Davis. She said they had evening classes at the Polytechnic. (*He pauses*) She said I ought to go.

Lily (*after a pause*) Do you suggest we overcharge you here?

Mr Davis. No—no. Five shillings an hour: it's very reasonable.

Lily. We do it as a favour.

Mr Davis. Yes.

Lily. You find me unsympathetic then?

Mr Davis. No.

Lily. Incompetent? You have lost faith in my coaching.

Mr Davis (*desperately*) But you don't teach me *movement*.

Sonny. We have to keep him sweet, that boy. It's important. With the anniversary coming up, I don't know what we should do.

Iris. We've nothing to pawn.

SONNY. There's the coffee lace.
LILY (*calling quietly*) Miss Fellowes!
IRIS. She won't part with it.
LILY (*calling*) Miss Fellowes.

(ROSE *and* JIMMY *react upstairs,* IRIS *and* SONNY *across the hall*)

IRIS. I won't be called twice in an hour. It's too much. I shan't go.
JIMMY. It's Iris. She wants Iris again.
ROSE. She goes too far. We're not servants.

(JIMMY *opens the door of the upstairs room, and listens*)

MR DAVIS. Shall I go and knock on the door? She may be deaf.
LILY. She is not deaf. She is in excellent health. (*Calling*) Miss Fellowes!
SONNY. Go along, dear.

(IRIS *goes into the main room*)

ROSE (*meanwhile*) What is it?
JIMMY. She wants Iris again. She's calling Iris.
ROSE. If it's important, we should all go.
JIMMY. She'll call if it's important.

(IRIS *enters Lily's room*)

IRIS. Well?
LILY. Mr Davis wishes to be taught dramatic movement.
MR DAVIS. I thought—if I could feel at ease.
IRIS (*to Mr Davis*) You've got a gap in your teeth, do you know that? You get that fixed, if you want to feel at ease. I mean, it stands to reason; you're self-conscious, aren't you?
MR DAVIS. I thought—if I could move dramatically.
IRIS. You can't keep moving all the time. They're bound to notice it, the moment you stop.

(SONNY *folds the blouse and puts it on the table* C)

LILY. I'd deal with it myself, but I am ill, as you know.
IRIS. Indigestion!
LILY (*warns*) Iris!

(MR DAVIS, *embarrassed, puts the book on the table down* R)

IRIS (*to Mr Davis*) She gets pains in her stomach, and calls it illness.
LILY (*with control*) The pains in my upper abdomen are nothing to do with Mr Davis, dear. He is not a medical man.
IRIS (*to Mr Davis*) Pains! (*Showing her hand*) You see that hand? On a wet day, it takes me five minutes to straighten the fingers. I've cried—cried with that hand.
LILY. Iris . . .

Iris (*to Lily*) And Sonny with his kidneys, standing there in the toilet for half an hour together.

(Sonny *begins to listen to the argument*)

Lily. Iris!

Iris. You could get up out of that bed, and take Mr Davis into our room for his lessons. He's got his overcoat. He doesn't need the fire. It's wind: that's all it is. You get wind, and call it pains, and we suffer.

Lily (*thundering*) I am to have tests for my pains.

(Jimmy *and* Sonny *hear this.* Sonny *stands up and comes to the hall*)

Mr Davis. I better go. (*After a pause*) I've had my hour. I've learned a lot. (*He stands behind the door*)

(*In the hall,* Sonny *makes up his mind to go in. He squares his shoulders and makes an entrance*)

Sonny (*with lots of attack*) Hullo, dears. (*He moves* c) Hullo, Mr Davis, dear. Enjoying yourself, are you? That's right.

Mr Davis (*moving to Sonny*) I've just finished.

Lily. I asked your wife for assistance with . . .

Iris. You never asked. You said you were ill. That's all.

Lily. She became unpleasant over my pains.

Iris. I was cold.

Lily. Mr Davis required help.

Sonny. What sort of help?

Mr Davis. I thought with dramatic movement.

Sonny. Dancing! We can do that. (*Demonstrating with a little dance*) Sonny Lynn and Iris Fellowes—we could teach him the elements. Tap, Soft-shoe. (*To Mr Davis*) Not ballet. We didn't *do* ballet. You've got a gap in your teeth, Mr Davis, dear. You ought to have it fixed. No, we did a lot with canes. We did formation dancing. We never did ballet.

Mr Davis. There was a lady did it on the wireless.

Sonny (*taking his arm and leading him into the corridor and then into the other room*) So she may, so she may, Mr Davis dear, but if you can't see her, you don't know if she's doing it right. Come along, Iris dear, we'll just go into the other room with the piano, and teach Mr Davis a little routine. Then he can practise at home in front of a mirror.

Iris (*to Lily*) We'll need the light on in the other room. (*She goes over to the gas fire and switches it out*) You know the rule.

Lily. But I'm an invalid. I require care.

Iris. If you've got a temperature, you don't need the fire. (*Calling*) You can turn the light on, Sonny. The fire's out here. (*She moves to the door*)

(Sonny *turns on the light and opens the lid of the piano*)

Sonny. Now isn't that cosy, Mr Davis dear. But you'd better keep your coat on till we warm you up.

(Iris *goes through to the other room*)

Mr Davis. I didn't know you had a piano.

Sonny. You would if we lived on the ground floor, Mr Davis dear. You'd have had it in your pawnshop. (*He finds a song in the piano stool*) Iris dear, you remember this?

Iris (*taking the music*) You don't expect me to play the piano with my arthritis.

Sonny. I wasn't asking you to play, dear. Just if you remembered it. (*To Mr Davis*) You'll enjoy this one, Mr Davis, dear. (*He plays a note on the piano*) There's the note.

(Iris *sits at the piano and tries the note.* Sonny *moves the table and fire below the piano.* Jimmy *and* Rose *listen*)

Rose. They're playing the piano.

Jimmy. They're never.

Rose. I heard it.

Jimmy. They're not playing now.

Rose. Listen, cleversticks.

Sonny (*moving l to Mr Davis*) I'm going to teach you something very simple to start with, Mr Davis dear.

Mr Davis (*bewildered*) Movement?

Sonny. That's right, dear, simple movement. (*Demonstrating*) We'll do one two three kick, and then back.

Mr Davis. Back.

Sonny. And then one two three kick again. I'll do it with you, and Iris will sing. Unless you'd rather play the piano, Iris dear. Do your *fingers* good.

Iris. I'll sing.

Sonny. Right. With me. (*He points out front*) There's the audience. Smile, Mr Davis dear. Big smile.

(Sonny *and* Mr Davis *dance, their hands on each other's shoulders like Tiller Girls*)

Iris (*sings*)	Sonny.
Over my	One two three
shoulder goes	Out you go
one care	Back now.
Over my	One two three
shoulder go	Kick again.
two cares	That's right.

(Rose *and* Jimmy *listen.* Lily *pulls the bedclothes over her head. The dance continues in silence*)

Rose. Iris is singing.

Jimmy. That's the television next door.

Rose (*rising and moving to her door*) I'm going down.

Jimmy. They'll think you want something.

Rose. Well, I do. I want to know what's going on.

(Rose *begins to come down.* Jimmy *stays where he is.* Sonny *now goes on with the routine, the first two lines having been repeated in silence during the last five lines*)

Sonny. You're not knock-kneed, Mr Davis dear, are you?

(Mr Davis *shakes his head, still smiling*)

No? Well, that's very good. Very good indeed. Now we'll do the next two. Iris? (*He demonstrates a side-step*)

(Rose *enters the room*)

Rose. Has he gone?

Mr Davis (*dancing, but badly*) Good evening, Miss Deveraux. We're doing dramatic movement.

Rose (*to Sonny*) He's got a gap in his teeth. Somebody should tell him.

Sonny. We have, dear; we all have. Come along, Mr Davis dear. Watch me. Iris?

(Iris *sings the next two lines, and* Sonny *bends his knees in time to the music, watched by* Rose *and* Mr Davis. *Next door,* Lily *emerges from beneath the bedclothes, sits up and listens*)

Sonny. Do you think you could do that, Mr Davis dear. Rose dear, I finished your blouse. It's on the table.

Rose (*taking the blouse from the table and moving to Sonny*) Oh, Sonny, you are good to me,

Iris. Are we going on or aren't we?

Rose (*showing the blouse to Mr Davis*) Isn't that nice, Mr Davis? Isn't it lovely.

(Sonny *helps* Rose *to put on the blouse*)

Mr Davis. Very attractive.

Rose. I've always liked bright colours. (*With a look at Iris*) You can wear bright colours or you can't. Something glittery; I can't resist it.

Iris (*singing*) *Why* should I . . .

Rose. No, Iris. He can't get the beat with you singing. He needs the piano.

Iris. I'm not playing the piano with my arth . . .

Rose. Nobody's asking you, Iris. We wouldn't expect it. Jimmy can play. (*He goes to the door and calls*) Jimmy! Come down, you're wanted.

Jimmy. If I'm wanted, I'll come. (*He turns off the fire and light and comes downstairs*)

Rose. You're to play the piano.

(Lily, *unable to bear this, gets out of bed. She goes to the door of her room, hesitates with her hand on the handle, then changes her mind. She goes to the wardrobe and gets a large old-fashioned hat with a ribbon. She tries it on, in front of the mirror.* MR DAVIS *takes off his overcoat and puts it on the chair down* L)

SONNY. Come along, Jimmy dear. You know the tune. Give him the music, Iris dear. Now, Mr Davis dear, we'll do it together. Rose, dear. Iris. All together. We're the boys, Mr Davis dear, and they're the girls. Jimmy!

(JIMMY *begins to play, and the three perform their routine, along with* MR DAVIS. *The routine is repeated,* MR DAVIS *encouraged. In the other room,* LILY *takes the centre of the stage, prepares herself, then begins a routine of her own. So we have four and the piano in one room,* LILY *dancing and singing by herself in a big hat in the other. The door from downstairs opens.* JOHNNY *enters. He is wearing an overcoat, very worn. He carries a bundle of papers and magazines. He comes into the corridor, stops on hearing the noise, listens. Then he opens the door to the large room quietly.* LILY *does not see him. She continues to sing and dance. As she reaches the end of the chorus, she strikes an attitude)*

SONNY (*breathless*) Very nice, Mr Davis dear. You do pick things up.

(JOHNNY *puts his papers on the bed and applauds.* LILY *turns to see him. She takes a step towards him. Then the pain hits her—a sharp pain in the upper stomach)*

LILY. Pain.

(*In the next room they all freeze. From now on, the coaching of* MR DAVIS *continues only intermittently, freezing into a still picture when not wanted.*)

(JOHNNY *helps* LILY *to sit on the foot of the bed)*

JOHNNY. Tum-tum, is it?

(LILY *nods*)

(*feels in his pocket*) Brought you some Settlers. (*Two lines of music are heard from the next room.* Rehearsing? (*He turns on the light then lights the gas fire*)

LILY. They are teaching Mr Davis dramatic movement.

SONNY. Smile, Mr Davis dear. Big smile. That's right.

LILY. Sonny says we should keep him sweet in view of the anniversary.

JOHNNY. Yes. (*A pause*) That's true, dammit. (*A pause*) Oh damn, and blast, and hell.

LILY. You were not successful?

JOHNNY. No luck. No luck at all. (*He sits on the foot of the bed beside Lily*) I go out every morning, and come back with nothing but mags. Nothing we can sell.

LILY. Johnny, you must not doubt yourself. If *you* were to doubt, we should all surrender, Johnny.

JOHNNY. I could be here, looking after you, instead of riding round and round on a damned underground train, hoping to find lost property. (*A pause*) Lil . . .

Lily. Yes?

Johnny. Old doctor came, eh?

Lily. I am to have tests. I told Iris so, but she is a grudging woman. You should not have brought home the *Readers' Digest*. Since reading it she has become a medical authority. Indigestion! "I might have an ulcer," I said to her, "and where would you all be then without my leadership?"

Johnny. It's not an ulcer, Lil.

Lily. Why should it not be?

Johnny. Too high up. My old dad had an ulcer. Bound to, I suppose, working on the Stock Exchange. And then I was a worry to him. Used to get this gnawing pain before meals. Everything boiled, and no lettuce. Ghastly life.

Lily. Well, I am to have tests.

(*There is a pause.* Johnny *finds difficulty in looking at her*)

Johnny. He didn't give you any idea what sort of tests?

Lily. It is not cancer, Johnny, if that is what you fear.

(Johnny *rises, takes off his coat, hangs it on the hooks* R, *then goes into the kitchen alcove to make tea.* Jimmy *plays the piano and* Rose *does a little dance of her own. The others applaud*)

Rose. We'll have to stop. I'm quite out of breath. (*She sits on the foot of the bed*)

(Iris *sits down* L. Sonny *moves above the piano stool.* Mr Davis *stands* c, *facing front, with a fixed grin on his face*)

Sonny (*to Iris*) He's very good, isn't he? You're very good, Mr Davis dear. Picks it up very quickly. It's all right, Mr Davis dear; you can stop smiling now.

Jimmy. He's got a gap in his teeth. He'll never make a juvenile.

Sonny. Never mind, dear. Never *mind*, Jimmy dear.

Jimmy (*moving to Mr Davis*) Comedy; that should be your aim. You should do comedy. Shouldn't he do comedy, Rosie?

Sonny. We'll teach him comedy next week.

Mr Davis. I wouldn't mind doing comedy.

Jimmy. I'll teach you. Comic patter. Jokes. Falling. We'll go into the big room with the fire.

Rose (*rising to* R *of Jimmy*) I don't want you to fall, Jimmy. I don't want you to do falling.

Sonny. He'll do the falling, dear. Jimmy won't fall.

Mr Davis. That's right. I don't mind falling.

Rose (*pulling Jimmy* R; *gently and protectively*) Well, you're not to let my husband fall. He's got bones like a bird, very fine and brittle. (*To Jimmy*) You were laid up last year with that wrist. I won't have you falling.

JIMMY. That wasn't falling. That was opening a bottle of bubbly.

MR DAVIS. Champagne?

IRIS. Only for the anniversary. We don't drink it as a rule.

MR DAVIS. Anniversary?

SONNY. The very first time we ever appeared on the West End stage, Mr Davis dear. The sixteenth of February, nineteen-twenty-four. It was the opening night of *Dancing With Daisy*.

JIMMY. We were in the chorus.

IRIS. You have to start in the chorus. You'll find that.

MR DAVIS. I was telling Miss Terralozzi. The vicar was asking if you'd do a turn at the Senior Citizens'.

IRIS. Go out?

MR DAVIS. There's a Gala Evening for the new premises.

IRIS (*rising*) We don't go out.

SONNY (*rising*) We would, Mr Davis dear. We would. But we don't.

ROSE. We don't like going out.

JIMMY. Not out of doors. (*He turns to the piano and sits*)

MR DAVIS. Miss Terralozzi said the fee wasn't big enough for artistes of your stature.

(JIMMY *picks out the first few notes of* "*Over My Shoulder*" *with one finger*)

SONNY (*changing the subject*) Better put your coat back on, Mr Davis dear. You don't want to catch a chill after all that dancing.

JOHNNY (*moving from the kitchen into the room* L) He's had more than his time, Lil. They'll be missing him at the shop. Won't do much good teaching him dramatic movement, if he gets the old heave-ho. (*He moves into the passage*) Ding dong! Ding dong! School's out.

(*The others react to his voice:* "*Johnny,*" "*It's Johnny,*" "*Johnny's back.*" MR DAVIS *puts on his coat.* JOHNNY *enters the room* R)

'Morning, Mr Davis. I saw Mr Simon as I came by the shop. He was standing in the doorway, looking worried.

MR DAVIS (*with a quick look at his watch*) I'm late.

ROSE. Johnny's not wearing a hat.

(SONNY *and* IRIS *react to this, realizing he has not had a successful day on the Underground*)

MR DAVIS. We've been doing dramatic movement.

ROSE. Where's your hat, Johnny? Did you take it off?

MR DAVIS. If you've got a hat, I'll take it with me, if you like.

(JOHNNY *shakes his head. They are all watching*)

Or anything in that line.

JOHNNY. Nothing in that line. You cut along now, eh, old son? Tell Mr Simon I kept you, if you like. On a business matter.

MR DAVIS. That's all right, Mr Sims: (*moving to the door*) I shan't

B

get into trouble. (*He moves into the passage*) Don't worry about me. It's hard to get assistants these days. He has to give me the latitude. (*Calling*) Good-bye, Miss Terralozzi. Thank you.

(Sonny, *sorry to see Mr Davis go, moves to the door to watch*)

Lily (*calling*) Come again on Thursday.
Mr Davis. Thursday.
Lily. I shall be stronger.
Davis. Thursday, then. (*Going*) Good-bye, all.

(Mr Davis *exits up* r)

Sonny. Such a sweet boy! (*He moves back into the room*)
Iris. Nothing, Johnny?
Johnny. Not a sausage. (*He moves into the corridor*)
Sonny (*following*) It's not sausages we need, Johnny dear. It's bowler hats. (*He passes Johnny and enters the room* l)
Jimmy (*following*) I wouldn't mind a sausage. I haven't had a sausage for a long time.

(Iris *turns off the light in the room* r)

Sonny. Or a good-class umbrella.

(Rose *and* Iris *follow the men*)

Iris. Despatch-case. If it's real leather.
Jimmy. I'd fancy a sausage. Chipolatas. I often think of them.

(*In the room* l, Jimmy *sits on the pouffe* r *of the fire*, Sonny *on the floor beside the fire*, Iris *brings the stool down* c *and sits* c, Rose *sits at Jimmy's feet.* Johnny *follows the others in and closes the door*)

Lily. Johnny was not successful. He had ill fortune.
Iris. He's told us.
Johnny (*standing by the door*) I got some mags, you know. And the papers.
Rose. Oh, he got the magazines.
Iris. You should have taken the Bakerloo Line. I keep telling you, but you won't listen. You're obstinate, Johnny.
Jimmy. He should have gone back to East Acton. There was that bag of groceries at East Acton.
Iris. Lightning never strikes twice in the same place. Stanmore, Dollis Hill, Wembley—it's a wealthy area: you could get anything there. Gloves—chiffon scarves—handbags . . .

(Johnny *moves up stage*)

Jimmy. He doesn't like handbags.
Sonny (*rising and moving* r) They're not lucky for you, Johnny dear. Not handbags. Remember when you sat on that handbag all the way from Tufnell Park to Tooting, and there was nothing in it but a bus ticket?

IRIS. There was no need to sit that long. He wasn't hatching it. (*To Johnny*) You were nervous: that's all.

JOHNNY (*bringing the papers and putting them on the table down* R) I don't like handbags, Iris. It feels like stealing. (*He stands above Iris*)

ROSE (*rising*) Did you get me *The Lady*, Johnny? (*She goes to the table and finds "The Lady"*)

IRIS. Did you get the *Reader's Digest?*

ROSE (*standing above the table*) I was reading the advertisements. There's a lovely guest-house in Ilfracombe. Refined religious family with cream teas. (*She sits as before*)

LILY. I won't have Iris reading the *Digest*. She gets notions.

SONNY (*picking up the "Evening Standard" from the table*) I'll just take the *Standard*, dear. Unless you've got anything in *my* line, Johnny dear. I once found a book of artistic poses inside a bush in Holland Park, but that was in the old days. You never get them left in the Tube. (*He moves down* L *and sits*)

ROSE. What are we going to do for the anniversary? Sonny was saying champagne.

IRIS. He can take the Bakerloo tomorrow.

ROSE (*rising*) There's not much time. (*She sits* L *on the foot of the bed*)

JOHNNY. Iris, I can't take the Bakerloo. Not first thing. I've got to be in the City at ten-thirty.

LILY. I told that boy your work took you to the City.

JOHNNY (*moving* L *of Iris*) Lil, he knows. (*He takes an Underground map from his pocket*) Look, old girl, Kennington at eight-thirty, right? Fourpenny ticket. North to Euston.

IRIS. You don't need to go to Euston. You could take the Bakerloo to Wembley.

JOHNNY. Not so *early*, Iris. North to Euston. Back to Warren Street. Goodge Street: you get the shop assistants at Heals, leaving their knitting.

IRIS. Sonny never did finish that knitting.

SONNY. I couldn't, dear. I didn't have the pattern.

JOHNNY. *There's* your gloves—Goodge Street, Tottenham Court Road, Leicester Square—across to Piccadilly Circus, Oxford Circus —there's your Liberty scarves. Then the Central Line to the City— bowler hats, umbrellas, brief-cases, *The Investors' Chronicle*.

(IRIS *grunts*)

There's no latitude until eleven o'clock. After that, you can make a choice.

IRIS. You didn't have to choose the District Line. There's money in Bushey.

JOHNNY. It's a long way, Iris. Bushey—Watford—it takes all morning. Anyway it's swings and roundabouts, old girl. People are more careless in Ladbroke Grove than they are in Watford.

IRIS. And what do you get there? Curry powder and green peppers. We've got to have something to sell.

Johnny. Well, I'm sorry.

Jimmy (*rising and moving to Johnny*) Johnny—what are we going to do, then?

Iris. Johnny must go out again.

Lily. I won't have Johnny under pressure.

Iris. We *are* under pressure.

Sonny (*reading the paper*) Oooh! Very saucy!

(Johnny *goes behind the screen to fetch tea.* Jimmy *sits on the pouffe*)

Lily. What?

Sonny. Nothing, Lily dear. Just an advert. Just reading the Personal Column.

Rose (*looking over his shoulder*) Let me see. Hold it higher. I can't read.

Iris. If you won't wear glasses, what do you expect?

Johnny (*looking round the screen*) What is it, Rosie?

Rose (*reading*) "Life in Death. Preserve your Loved Ones and We Will Pay. Limited Offer Only."

Lily. Americans!

Rose. No, no, Lily. It's in the *Standard*.

Lily. Give it to me. (*She takes the paper and reads*) There! "From London, Ohio, to London, England. Knight's Embalming Service Brings Life-in-Death to the British People". Of course it's Americans. Who else could it be?

Johnny (*coming down with a tray of cups and mugs of tea, and a bottle and glass of milk*) What's Life-in-Death?

Lily. Embalming. Filthy habit. (*She gives the paper back to Sonny*)

Sonny (*reading*) "With Life-in-Death Even the Remotest Relatives May Pay Their Last Respects Without Offensive Odours."

Rose. Odours?

Sonny. Stops you going bad, dear. (*Reading*) "Lead-lined Coffins Allow Loved Ones to Look Their Best When Meeting Their Maker on That Final Day."

Johnny. What did it mean?—they'll *pay*. (*He puts the tray on the table down* R)

Sonny. Wait a minute: I'm trying to find it. (*He finds it*) Oh, it's a school. They're running a school to train people to do it, and they need bodies. Fifteen pounds each. There you are, Johnny dear, if you could find a body on the Bakerloo, we'd have ever such a nice anniversary.

Johnny (*giving tea to Iris*) I suppose we couldn't . . .

Iris. What?

Johnny. Postpone the anniversary? (*He moves back to the table*)

(*They all look at him*)

Have it later?

Lily (*after a pause*) Johnny, my dear, it *wasn't* later.

Iris. February the sixteenth.

ROSE (*breaking down and beginning to cry*) Nineteen-twenty-four.

(*General concern*)

SONNY. Rosie dear!

IRIS. Rose!

ROSE (*rising from the bed and crossing below it to up* C; *weeping*) I can't help it. Just thinking of it. I was so pretty. I was always the pretty one.

SONNY. You *are* the pretty one, dear. You're the pretty one, and Iris is the handsome one . . .

LILY. And *I* am the beautiful one. Go to her, Jimmy. Johnny, console her.

(JIMMY *goes to Rose and stands by her, helpless.* JOHNNY *pats her head*)

JOHNNY. There there, eh? There, there, dammit!

ROSE. I was a little butterfly. A little moth. (*To Johnny; indignantly*) We've got the coldest room in the house, and now you say we can't have the anniversary party.

(JIMMY *sits on the pouffe*)

JOHNNY. I didn't say we couldn't have it. Just postpone it. (*He picks up two teacups from the table*)

SONNY (*rising and going to collect the tea from Johnny*) It's not the same, Johnny dear. If you start letting things slide, you end up with nothing. It's not the time to speak of it, dear, but we have all made sacrifices.

JIMMY. That's right.

SONNY (*giving Rose a cup and retaining the other*) If I'd played my cards right, if I hadn't been loyal and true to my friends . . .

IRIS. He wanted to keep you, that man. That's all.

SONNY. I could have been someone, dear.

IRIS. You'd have been kept.

SONNY. I'd have had chances made for me, Iris dear. Opportunities of all sorts.

(IRIS *snorts*)

But I was loyal, dear. I wouldn't break us up. (*He sits* L)

IRIS (*to Johnny*) You can't postpone it.

LILY. That will do, Iris.

(JOHNNY *gives a glass of milk to Lily*)

IRIS. Well, we can't.

LILY. *I* shall tell my husband what he can and can't do, if you don't mind. (*To Johnny*) You can't postpone it. An anniversary is on the day, or it is nothing. One doesn't postpone Christmas. One keeps it on the day Christ chose to be born.

SONNY. We'll just have to pawn something.

JOHNNY. What?

(*There is a pause.* IRIS *goes to the table and pours more milk in her tea*)

IRIS. There's the coffee lace.

LILY. Out of the question.

IRIS. We pawned it before.

LILY. Once. In the most dire emergency.

IRIS. It's an emergency now.

LILY. You're too quick, Miss Fellowes. You're too quick with the property of others.

SONNY. Share and share alike, Lily dear.

LILY. I will share a great deal, Sonny. I shall not share my clothes.

JOHNNY. We got twelve pounds for it before, my dear.

JIMMY. We could buy a lot with twelve pounds. We could buy sausages—a pie . . .

ROSE. Champagne.

LILY (*rising and picking up her hat*) I will not pawn my coffee lace for your anniversary. (*She hangs her hat in the wardrobe up* L)

SONNY. *Our* anniversary, dear.

JOHNNY (*after a pause*) We did get twelve quid, Lil. He gives more when he knows we're going to redeem it.

JIMMY. That's right.

JOHNNY. Last time we had it out again within the week.

LILY. That was ten years ago. Our circumstances have changed.

IRIS. If Johnny wasn't so nervous with handbags, we shouldn't be in this position.

JOHNNY. I won't go to prison, Iris.

IRIS. You don't like to be seen carrying one; that's all. You're afraid of what people might think.

LILY. Johnny is not to go to prison. He is not to be put at risk. I must remind you, Miss Fellowes, that my husband is the business manager here. He has always looked after us. We depend on him. I remind you of that.

ROSE. You ought to apologize to Johnny. He works very hard.

JIMMY. We wouldn't know what to do without Johnny, Iris.

(*There is a pause.* IRIS *is ashamed, but defiant*)

IRIS. I won't apologize. (*She leaves the room and goes and sits on the stairs*)

(*The others look at one another*)

LILY. Sonny!

(SONNY *rises and moves* R)

JOHNNY. No. I'll go. (*He goes to Iris in the hall*)

LILY. Temperamental little thing!

(JOHNNY *stands looking at* IRIS, *who will not look round*)

Johnny. Make it up, eh?
Iris. I shan't say I'm sorry.
Johnny. Don't need to, old girl. We know it.

(Iris *turns to him and he comforts her*)

Never been any good with handbags. I haven't the art of it, old
girl.
Iris. You should try—the Bakerloo.
Johnny. Try it tomorrow.
Iris. There's money on the Bakerloo, Johnny.
Johnny. Come in now, eh? Come back to the fire.
Iris. We'll have to pawn the coffee lace.
Johnny. She knows.

(*They move to the room* l)

Sonny (*moving to Lily*) It'll have to be the coffee lace, Lily dear.
We all know it.
Lily. But what shall I wear?
Sonny. I'll think of something, dear.

(Iris *and* Johnny *return.* Iris *moves down* r, Johnny rc)

Lily's decided to pawn the coffee lace, dear. (*He sits on the bed*) You'd
better take it round straight away. We've done a lot of work on that
boy today. He ought to give us a good price.
Johnny. Thought I'd try the Bakerloo tomorrow.
Lily. If you take it now, Mr Davis will be alone in the shop.
Jimmy. Twelve quid we got last time.
Sonny. I hope he gives us more than that. You won't get much
bubbly for twelve pounds.
Lily. We shall make the list while you are away, and you can
visit the shops after your nap.

(Lily *gives her glass to* Jimmy, *who puts it on the table.* Lily *goes to
the wardrobe and takes out a very old-fashioned coffee-lace evening dress on
its hanger*)

Tell Mr Davis I shall require him to care for the dress while it is in
his charge. Impress on him, Johnny: he must take great care. (*She
gives Johnny the dress*)

(*The doorbell rings. They all look at one another. After a moment the
bell rings again*)

Lily. Go on, Johnny.

(Johnny *gives the dress back to Lily and goes into the hall to answer the
door. The others listen*)

Johnny (*at the door up* r) Who is it?
Mr Davis (*off*) It's me. Mr Davis.
Rose. Who? Who?

(JOHNNY *opens the door*)

SONNY. It's Mr Davis, dear.
MR DAVIS. The vicar dropped in.
LILY. Johnny!
JOHNNY. Excuse me. (*He goes back to the others*)
LILY. Shut the door.

(JOHNNY *does so*)

(*Giving him the dress*) Strike while the iron is hot.
JOHNNY. Righty old ho. (*He rejoins Mr Davis in the corridor*)
MR DAVIS. I came to tell you about the vicar.
LILY (*calling*) Negotiate, Johnny. Negotiate.
MR DAVIS. The vicar said . . .

(JOHNNY *takes* MR DAVIS *into the room* R *and closes the door*)

JOHNNY. No time for that now, old son. (*He turns on the light*)
MR DAVIS. He said . . .
JOHNNY. First things first. Got something for you here.
DAVIS. For me?
LILY (*sitting on the foot of the bed*) And now, Sonny, if you'll get a paper and pencil, we shall make a list.

(SONNY *finds a piece of paper and pencil in the dressing-table drawer then sits* R *of Lily on the bed*)

JOHNNY. Coffee lace. A good colour. *Café au lait.*
MR DAVIS (*examining the dress*) It's been worn, of course.
JOHNNY. It's been worn to the opera.
MR DAVIS. Yes—worn.
JOHNNY. It's been worn before King Edward the Eighth, Mr Davis. Before Edward the Eighth, the Duke of Windsor, while he was still the Prince of Wales.

(*In Lily's room,* SONNY *makes a list.* ROSE *kneels on the bed up stage of Lily and Sonny.* JIMMY *rises and looks over Sonny's shoulder*)

LILY. A glass of dry sherry before the meal. Champagne with.
ROSE. That's right, Sonny. I fancy a glass of sherry.
JIMMY. I haven't tasted sherry . . .
LILY. We had sherry in nineteen-fifty-three. A glass of dry sherry before dinner. Each.
IRIS. The price has gone up. They raise it every year with the Budget.
SONNY. South African's cheaper, dear. Or Australian. There was that lovely Australian we met in the war, doing one-night stands at Manipur Road. Digger, his name was.
LILY. I don't think anyone here would expect me to drink Australian sherry. And a roast of some sort. Beef or veal.
ROSE. Veal's a very *white* meat.

JIMMY. Veal's tasteless. You can't taste veal.

IRIS. Expensive. A leg of lamb; that's better.

LILY. *Contrefilet de boeuf* with roast potatoes and haricots verts. Write it down, Sonny.

SONNY (*writing*) Roast beef and beans . . .

MR DAVIS (*to Johnny*) It's ten years older.

JOHNNY. Prices have gone up in ten years. You should give more.

MR DAVIS. It's had ten years' more wear.

JOHNNY. Nonsense! Once a year on the anniversary; that's all. It's in beautiful condition.

MR DAVIS. An evening dress—you want it new, Mr Sims. This is more than thirty years old, by your own account.

JOHNNY. We shall redeem it. Twenty-five pounds is nothing for a dress like that.

MR DAVIS. But how can you redeem twenty-five pounds? Not without some careless person leaves his wage packet in the Tube.

JOHNNY (*after a pause*) Very well. Fifteen.

LILY. It's more than doubled in value. We shall allow thirty pounds to be safe.

IRIS. We can't spend thirty pounds on a meal. It's wicked.

ROSE. It's the anniversary, Iris.

LILY. We've had a great deal more than thirty pounds spent on our meals before this. A great deal more, and by Johnny for one.

IRIS. Not lately.

ROSE. Johnny never stinted. Not when he had the money.

JIMMY. We should have that first supper again, Lily. That first one, when the waiter signed the menu. I'd like to have that again.

ROSE. That's right.

JIMMY. Johnny stood treat.

ROSE. Oh, he loved you then, Lily. He spent a lot.

LILY. He loves me now.

JIMMY. Oysters. We had a dozen oysters. I haven't tasted oysters . . .

LILY. With the champagne.

JIMMY. And beef.

LILY. *Contrefilet de boeuf.* As I suggested.

JIMMY (*to Iris*) Roast beef. All bloody. That's what we had.

LILY. With burgundy. You'd better put down a bottle of burgundy, Sonny, and Johnny shall warm it by the fire. We're sure to finish the champagne with the oysters.

SONNY. But we're not having oysters.

LILY. Nonsense. Of course we're having oysters. Put down oysters. We can get the man at the fish shop to come round and open them. Sonny read the list.

SONNY (*reading*) One bot Spanish sherry . . .

LILY. Dry.

SONNY. Dry. (*Reading*) Two bots champagne.

IRIS. *Non*-vintage.

(LILY *makes a dismissive gesture*)

SONNY (*reading*) Six dozen oysters. One Hovis loaf. One pound butter. Three lemons. Three pounds fillet of beef. Three pounds potatoes. Pound and a half French beans.

IRIS. They're out of season.

LILY. They can be bought.

MR DAVIS (*to Johnny*) I'll give you four pound ten.

(*There is a pause.* JOHNNY *sits down* L)

JOHNNY. I can't tell them. It's too humiliating.

IRIS (*to Lily*) Anyway, I thought you had indigestion.

LILY. I have pains, Iris.

(JIMMY *sits on the pouffe*)

ROSE. In her upper stomach.

LILY. You know that.

IRIS. Wind!

SONNY. That's enough, Iris dear.

LILY. *Good* food is never indigestible. Oysters digest themselves. If you were more accustomed to high life, you would not need to be told.

MR DAVIS (*to Johnny*) But you could have a lovely anniversary for four pound ten. Bridge rolls. A bottle of wine. A chicken from Sainsbury's with roast and sprouts. After Eight mints. Nescafé Superior Brew with the Gold Label. You could have a spread. Get an ice-cream gateau and keep it on the window-sill; I've known that done. Stone's Ginger Wine for afterwards; it's warming. And half a bottle of whiskey for a whiskey Mac.

JOHNNY. It's not enough, Mr Davis. They're used to the best.

MR DAVIS. You could have the best. I came to tell you. There's no need to pawn Miss Terralozzi's effects. You can have enough without it.

JOHNNY. I don't understand you.

MR DAVIS (*moving to the door*) The vicar. You diverted me with the dress. He stopped by. We spoke. He appreciates your point of view.

JOHNNY (*rising and following Mr Davis*) What point of view?

MR DAVIS. Eight-and-six. It's insulting to an artiste. He sees that. He's authorized me to increase the offer.

JOHNNY. For what?

MR DAVIS. Miss Terralozzi knows about it. They all do. (*He opens the door*) Excuse me. (*He crosses the hall*)

(JOHNNY *follows*)

(*Moving* R *of the bed*) It's all right, Miss Terralozzi. The vicar says he can run to ten. Miss Fellowes, Mr Lynn, I've been in negotiation. It's two guineas each.

LILY. Johnny?

JOHNNY. I can't follow him.

Lily. What does he offer for the coffee lace?
Johnny. Four pound ten.
Lily. Insulting!
Mr Davis. But I got you ten guineas, Miss Terralozzi. I mean, if
you want me to take the dress as well, that's extra. I wouldn't spend
fifteen pound on food myself.
Iris. Ten guineas for what?
Mr Davis. The Senior Citizens. I told you.

(*There is a pause*)

Rose (*moving down* l *of the bed; nervously*) We don't go out.
Mr Davis (*to Rose*) A professional appearance.
Lily. Tell him, Johnny.
Johnny. They don't go out, Mr Davis.
Mr Davis. You said yourself, Mr Sims. You need the money.
Sonny. We never go out.
Mr Davis (*to Sonny*) You're professionals.
Iris. We've retired.

(Rose *sits* l *of the bed*)

Mr Davis (*desperately*) It's not fair.
Johnny. What?
Mr Davis (*facing the group*) You ask twenty-five pound for a dress
not worth ten shillings. You go on at me about the Duke of Windsor
and King Edward the Eighth. You make me feel socially inferior,
Mr Sims; and I've done my best for you. Miss Terralozzi said eight
and six each was insulting. Well, I made representations for you,
out of my pure respect for you: I spoke very strongly. And all you
can do . . .
Johnny. Mr Davis . . .
Mr Davis. Spurn me; that's what you do. (*Moving down* r) You
spurn my endeavours.
Iris (*after a pause*) We can't go out.
Mr Davis (*turning on them*) Why?
Iris (*after a pause*) Tell him.
Lily (*rising and moving to Mr Davis*) After the war, Mr Davis, pro-
fessional work was not easy to come by. We had been out of the
country too long. People had taken advantage of our absence.
Nevertheless we persisted.
Iris. Crowd work.
Rose. Table Service at the Corner House.
Sonny. Dressing.
Jimmy. Fairground employment.
Lily. But we kept the act together. Though they were not
frequent, we still had bookings. We were never the top of the bill,
you understand, but we had our own public; we had our style.
The Three Posies, With Sonny and Jim. Mr Sims negotiated our
contracts.

Johnny. Don't, Lil. (*He sits* R *on the bed*)

Lily. No-one blames you, Johnny. No-one here blames you.

Mr Davis. You mean I should have let Mr Sims talk to the vicar?

Lily. We were approached by a Mr Wolf Flutter for an eight-week tour. It was an excellent offer, as it seemed. Mr Sims negotiated a fee. We were contracted. It was a time—you would not remember it, of course, but there used to be something called Rock and Roll.

Mr Davis. I've heard of it.

Lily. Our act was not of that sort. We made no concessions.

Mr Davis. I understand that, Miss Terralozzi.

Lily. The other acts *were* of that sort.

Mr Davis. You would have formed a contrast.

Iris. We formed the bloody comic relief.

Lily. Thank you, Iris; I shall tell the story. (*To Mr Davis*) We had been hired, as we discovered, to be mocked by adolescents.

Mr Davis. Teenagers.

Lily. If you prefer. On the opening night, finding the house difficult, we attempted to impose authority. We were unable to make ourselves heard. Personal expressions were used—laughter—people attempted to climb on to the stage . . .

(Rose *begins to sob*)

Be quiet, Rose. (*To Mr Davis*) At the end of the week, since we were all distressed, Mr Sims approached Mr Wolf Flutter and asked him to release us from our contract. He refused. It was then we discovered that we had been engaged for this very purpose. To be mocked. (*She pauses*) We played the eight-week tour, Mr Davis, and for the latter part of the week it was twice nightly. (*She pauses*) We have not appeared professionally since then. We lack the confidence. Nor do we go out. We make our own entertainment. We have our own world here. (*She pauses*) Johnny, will you continue your negotiations for the dress?

Mr Davis. I'll allow you five pound for the dress. (*He waits a moment*) I'm sorry. It's the highest I can go.

Mr Davis *turns and leaves the room as the lights fade and—*

the Curtain *falls*

SCENE 2

Scene—*The same. Night.*

When the Curtain *rises, the stage is very dimly lit.* Rose *and* Jimmy, Iris *and* Sonny, Lily *and* Johnny *are all asleep in their double beds.* Iris *is making little moaning noises in her sleep. After a few moments,*

SONNY *wakes, gets out of bed, looks for his slippers in the dark, puts them on, finds the overcoat on the hooks up* R *and puts it on. Underneath he is wearing long underwear and socks. He goes down the corridor into the lavatory, closing the door behind him.* IRIS *half wakes.*

IRIS. Sonny, Sonny! (*Realizing where he is*) Oh.

(*A loud snore from* JIMMY *wakes* ROSE)

ROSE. Jimmy, you're snoring. Stop it, Jimmy. Turn over. Don't lie on your back.

(ROSE *gives Jimmy a push. He stops snoring. There is a sound of shunting trains in the distance.* JIMMY *starts snoring again*)

Oh dear! Oh dear! I never sleep. I never get a wink of sleep.

(LILY *suddenly gives a loud cry. Silence. Then the lavatory door opens and* SONNY *puts his head out.* LILY *gives another cry, not so loud, then noises at the back of the throat, as if she were fighting for breath.* JOHNNY *wakes and sits up in bed*)

JOHNNY. What's the matter, Lil? (*He gets out of bed*) What's up, eh? Indigestion?

(LILY *makes more of the fighting-for-breath noises*)

ROSE. What is it, Jimmy?
JOHNNY. I'll turn the light on.
ROSE. Turn the light on. What's happened?
JIMMY. Bad dream. Somebody having a dream.

(LILY *gives another loud cry. Then she is dead.* JOHNNY *switches on the light.* SONNY *goes back into the lavatory and pulls the chain. Then he returns to the corridor and stands outside the door of the large room, uncertain whether to knock*)

JOHNNY. Lil? Lil? Lily, girl? (*He takes her hand*) It's all right, girl. Nothing to worry. All gone now. (*He pauses*) Lily?

(SONNY *knocks*)

SONNY. Johnny?
JOHNNY. What is it?
SONNY. Is everything all right, Johnny dear? Is Lily having a turn?
JOHNNY. I don't know. She doesn't speak.

(SONNY *enters the room*)

I'll have to go for the doctor.
SONNY. You get dressed, Johnny. I'll stay with her. (*He closes the door*)

(JOHNNY *is also wearing long underwear and socks. He takes his shirt and trousers from the chair down* L *and begins to put them on. Meanwhile*

IRIS *gets out of bed and switches on the light. The women also wear underclothes in bed.* IRIS *takes the second overcoat from the hooks and puts it on*)

JOHNNY. She doesn't speak. She doesn't answer.
SONNY (*moving to the bed*) She's had a turn, hasn't she? That's it.

(IRIS *joins them*)

IRIS. Is it Lily?
SONNY. She's had a turn. (*He shuts the door behind Iris*) It's her indigestion.
JOHNNY. It's her pains. She cried out. I turned the light on. I went to her. She doesn't answer.

(IRIS *goes to Lily and takes her hand*)

Shall I get a glass of water?
IRIS. She's dead.
JOHNNY. What? (*He moves L of the bed*)
IRIS. She's dead, Johnny.
JOHNNY. But she was to have . . . tests. Test for her pains.
IRIS. It was very quick, Johnny. It must have been very quick.

(SONNY *gets a mirror from the dressing-table and holds it to Lily's face.* JOHNNY *is watching him.* SONNY *looks across at Johnny after making the mirror test. For a moment the two of them look at each other*)

SONNY. It's true, Johnny.

(IRIS *goes to the door, steps into the corridor and calls upstairs*)

IRIS. Rose! Jimmy! Get dressed and come down. Lily's dead. (*She goes to the dressing-table and looks for matches*)

(ROSE *and* JIMMY *sit up in bed*)

ROSE (*to Jimmy*) What? What did Iris say?
JIMMY. She said Lil's dead. (*He switches on the light*)
ROSE. She can't of died.
JIMMY. She could. We all could. We're old.
ROSE. She couldn't. It makes the numbers wrong.
JIMMY. Get dressed, Iris said. We're to go down.

(ROSE *and* JIMMY *begin to dress.* IRIS *lights the gas fire*)

JOHNNY (*moving down* C) I ought to go for the doctor.
SONNY. That's right. We'll stay here. (*He gets Johnny's coat from the wardrobe up* L)
JOHNNY (*helpless*) They don't like to be called at night.
IRIS. You have to phone the doctor. That's the law. Have you got a sixpence?

(JOHNNY *feels in his pocket and nods*)

Go on, then.

JOHNNY (*hesitating*) You're sure . . . ? (*He takes a step towards the bed, and cries out*) Lil!

(SONNY *helps Johnny into his coat, takes his arm, and leads him into the corridor*)

SONNY. Go along, Johnny dear. You go and telephone. Give you something to do, dear. That's best.

(IRIS, *left alone, moves* L *of the bed, picks up Lily's slippers from under the bed and stands looking at them.* JOHNNY *exits up* R. SONNY *returns to the room* L)

IRIS. I never liked her, Sonny. Bossy interfering bitch! I'll miss her.

(JIMMY *turns off the light in his room.* ROSE *and* JIMMY *come down into the corridor*)

ROSE. Iris?
SONNY. In here, dear.

(ROSE *and* JIMMY *come in fearfully, each trying to push the other to go first, like two timid children. They look towards the bed, then away again.* ROSE *will not go near the body. She comes to the fire*)

ROSE. You've lit the fire. (*She sits on the pouffe*)
IRIS. Yes.
JIMMY (*moving* RC) Johnny's gone out.
IRIS. To phone the doctor.

(JIMMY *begins a curious half-sideways motion up stage. He wants to see the body, but he is afraid. He takes a quick peek.* IRIS *and* SONNY *watch.* ROSE *ignores him*)

Satisfied?
JIMMY (*coming down to Rose*) Lily's dead, Rosie.
ROSE. She can't die. I told you. It makes the numbers wrong. Lily's very strong. She's the strongest.
SONNY (*moving above Rose*) It was her pains, dear. Her pains killed her.
ROSE. If everybody dies, I'll be left alone. She can't die.
JIMMY. I'll be with you, Rosie.
SONNY. That's right, Rosie. Jimmy'll look after you.
JIMMY. I'm very strong. I get hungry sometimes, but I've always been strong.
IRIS (*moving to the door; to Sonny*) We'll get dressed.

(*They go towards their own room.* JIMMY *is alarmed*)

JIMMY. You're not going to leave us alone with her.
IRIS. Somebody's got to stay with her.
SONNY. We'll leave our door open.

(IRIS *and* SONNY *go into their own room, where they dress*)

JIMMY (*moving to Rose and speaking quickly*) Johnny'll have to have our room. We'll have Iris and Sonny's room. They'll come in here.
ROSE. Sssssh!
JIMMY. Iris'll have to give the lessons, and I'll teach falling.
ROSE. Sssssh, Jimmy!
JIMMY. He'll be very cold. Poor Johnny! It's a cold room, Rosie.
ROSE. You don't know she can't hear you.
JIMMY. What?
ROSE. You don't know the dead can't hear. Nobody knows. She could have her spirit, listening.

(JIMMY *looks at her, alarmed. Then he goes to the screen that encloses the kitchen area*)

JIMMY. Come and help me with this screen.

(*They move the screen so that it completely masks the bed.* JOHNNY *comes in from outside. He watches them for a short while, unnoticed*)

JOHNNY. What are you doing?
JIMMY. We thought she'd like the privacy.
SONNY (*calling*) Is that you, Johnny?
IRIS. Is it?

(SONNY *nods*)

IRIS (*joining Johnny*) Is the doctor coming?
JOHNNY. He said, tomorrow morning.
IRIS. But she's dead.
SONNY (*joining them*) Is the doctor . . . ?
IRIS. Tomorrow morning.
SONNY. But she's . . .
JOHNNY. He said, if she's dead there's no hurry.
ROSE (*moving to the chair down* L) What does he expect us to do? (*She sits*) Sitting here with Lily dead!

(JIMMY *moves down* L *to Rose*)

SONNY. He wouldn't take her away, dear. They don't do that. He takes a look, and writes a certificate.
JOHNNY. I don't want her taken away. Not yet. It's not respectful. This is her room.

(ROSE *and* JIMMY *exchange a look*)

JIMMY. Yes, it is.
JOHNNY. It's her own room while she's in it. I won't have Lily rushed.
ROSE. That's right. That's very right and proper.
JIMMY. Where are you going to sleep, Johnny?
IRIS. He'll sleep in the chair.

SONNY. Was it her pains, Johnny?

JOHNNY. Angina something. Chest pains. He was going to give her tests. He didn't tell her. He had to take the tests first, he said.

JIMMY. My father died of his chest. Asthma. He died in the fog.

ROSE. He died in the Chiswick Empire, your father.

JIMMY. They've pulled it down now.

JOHNNY. It was a heart attack.

JIMMY. No, it was asthma.

(SONNY *signals to Johnny not to say any more*)

JOHNNY. She had a heart attack. She wouldn't suffer, he said. He'll make the arrangements in the morning.

SONNY. What arrangements?

IRIS. Undertaker.

ROSE (*starting to cry*) Poor Lily! Poor Lily!

(JIMMY *looks helplessly at Johnny for guidance. Then he starts to cry as well*)

JOHNNY. Don't cry, Rose. Don't cry.

ROSE. Lily's dead! Poor Lily!

JIMMY (*bawling*) Lily's dead.

SONNY (*facing up stage*) Be quiet, Jimmy dear.

ROSE. She'll miss the anniversary.

(JIMMY *bawls louder*)

She always loved the anniversary. Sitting there at the head of the table in her coffee lace. Now she'll miss it.

IRIS (*hard*) Well, she won't be the only one.

(ROSE *and* JIMMY *stop crying at once*)

JIMMY. What?

IRIS. She won't be the only one. There won't *be* an anniversary.

JIMMY. Because of . . . (*He indicates the screen*) Because it's not respectful, Iris?

JOHNNY (*troubled*) Lil wouldn't have wanted that.

IRIS. Because there'll be no money.

JIMMY. But we've got the money. Johnny got it for the coffee lace.

IRIS. We'll have to pay the undertaker.

(*There is a pause. They take it in*)

ROSE. No anniversary?

IRIS. We've got to bury her.

JIMMY. No anniversary?

SONNY. Er . . .

JOHNNY. What?

SONNY. I had a thought.

IRIS. What thought?

SONNY. Just something I read, dear.

C

(After a pause. IRIS *realizes what Sonny has been thinking of)*

IRIS. No, Sonny, no!
SONNY. I never mentioned it. I never spoke my thought.
JOHNNY. What does he mean, Iris?
IRIS. Never mind.

(After a pause. ROSE *gets it)*

ROSE. Oooh! Yes, that's right.
IRIS. That's enough, Rose.
JOHNNY. Is it a secret? What are you . . . ?
JIMMY *(realizing)* It was in the paper. Sonny found it.
IRIS *(angrily)* Be quiet!
SONNY *(after a pause)* You've got to think of the living, Iris. Lily always did.

*(JOHNNY *looks at each of them. Then he realizes what thought is in their minds)*

JOHNNY. No. *(He moves* R)

*(JOHNNY *is about to leave the room, but* SONNY *stops him)*

SONNY. Lily always had large ideas. Oysters.
JIMMY. Roast beef.
ROSE *(rising)* Champagne. She said, champagne.
SONNY. Get the paper, Jimmy dear.

*(JIMMY *fetches the paper from the chair down* L. JOHNNY *turns to Iris, looking for reassurance)*

JOHNNY. Iris . . . ?
IRIS. Leave me out of it.
SONNY. When I think of all she hoped for! Green beans and cigars.

*(JIMMY *gives Sonny the paper)*

Thank you, Jimmy dear. *(To Johnny)* It was Lily started the anniversary, Johnny. It was her idea. She thought of it, and you paid for it.
JOHNNY. Yes. *(He moves below the pouffe)*
JIMMY. If it had been one of us passed away, what would Lily have done?
SONNY. No, Jimmy dear: that's the wrong way about. What would Lily want *for* us? What would *you* want, Johnny, if you'd passed away, dear? If the anniversary was coming, and you knew the opportunity, what would you want us to do?
ROSE. That's right.
JOHNNY *(after a pause)* Damn! *(He sits on the pouffe, facing down stage)*
IRIS *(moving above the pouffe)* It's different for Johnny. Johnny's always sacrificed himself for us.

SONNY. I'd like Lily to have a nice funeral. It's the least we can do. What would it cost, Iris dear? What could we get for five pound? Lily always liked to make a good appearance. I've often heard her say that. Rolls Royces. Top hats. You wouldn't get your Rolls Royces, dear, for five pound. You wouldn't get your mutes and your black crêpe. (*He turns to the advertisement and reads*) "A first-class headstone in glazed granite with appropriate remembrances handcarved, and coloured granite chips to cover the grave." (*To Johnny*) Chips! It's all included, Johnny. They include chips, dear.

JOHNNY (*after a pause*) You do what you want. I can't stop you.

SONNY. No, dear. You have to sign the form.

ROSE (*moving* C) Johnny's always looked after things. All the official things. Johnny manages us. We don't go out.

JOHNNY. Not this time.

SONNY. Do you think *we* didn't love her?

JOHNNY (*after a pause*) I know you did.

SONNY. All these years. We've had our share of quarrels, but we've stayed together, dear. We've had our laughs and our disagreements. We've split apart, and come together again, we've toured and we've shared, and we've stayed together. We've given up chances. We all have. Don't you think we didn't love her. She was one of us.

JOHNNY. I know you loved her. You don't have to remind me.

SONNY. And we love you too, Johnny. You do what *you* want.

JIMMY. She always liked the anniversary.

ROSE. She started it. Sonny said.

JOHNNY (*appealing*) Iris?

IRIS. Make up your own mind.

JOHNNY. But I've always—looked after you.

IRIS. Lily's told you what she wanted and you've done it. Now you've got to decide for yourself.

JOHNNY. You were artistic, and I looked after the practical side.

IRIS. You've been our slave for forty years.

SONNY (*after a pause*) That's not kind, dear.

IRIS. No, it's true.

SONNY. If you don't want the anniversary . . .

IRIS. I do want it.

JOHNNY. What?

IRIS. I do want it. It's what we live for. Something special once a year. Something to remember. But I want you to have respect, Johnny.

SONNY. He has respect.

JOHNNY. I have respect.

IRIS. No. We've relied on you. We've not respected you. You've not respected yourself. With Lily—with selling Lily . . .

SONNY. With the embalment.

IRIS. With selling Lily's body; that's what it is.

SONNY. With getting her a funeral, dear. A finer funeral than .. .

IRIS (*moving to Sonny; angrily*) I don't care. I don't care what happens to Lily. She's dead.

ROSE. Iris, she might hear you.

JOHNNY. Eh?

IRIS (*more gentle*) No, Johnny. She can't hear. She can't tell you what to do. She's dead. I always thought I didn't like her, but now I miss her. And you loved her: I know that. Working for her, working for us all, Johnny, you did it very willing; I know that. How we bury her—it doesn't make any difference to Lily. Selling her body to the Americans—that won't hurt her. And if we have the anniversary or not—that won't hurt her either. But you must do what *you* want, Johnny. (*Moving R of Johnny*) Decide for yourself and have respect.

JOHNNY. I can't change, Iris.

SONNY. Of course he won't. Johnny's been devoted to us all his life, dear. He won't change now.

IRIS. There's been a change.

JOHNNY. I have to think of what—she'd want.

SONNY. You know what she'd want, Johnny dear.

JIMMY. Lily always liked the anniversary.

ROSE. She started it.

IRIS (*after a pause*) Yes, you know what she'd want.

JOHNNY. I've got five pounds. We've not spent it. I'll go to Mr Davis in the morning.

JIMMY. Eh?

JOHNNY. For the coffee lace, Jimmy. (*Rising and turning to face them all*) If she's going into the hands of strangers, she must look her best.

(*The lights fade slowly to* BLACK-OUT.

After a few moments the lights come up again as before. LILY *lies on the bed, dressed in her coffee lace.* IRIS *and* ROSE *are making up her face,* ROSE *holding an old cigar-box of make-up.* JIMMY *is sitting on the pouffe,* SONNY *down* L)

IRIS. Take the screen away, Jimmy.

(JIMMY *rises and places the screen by the wall of the kitchen alcove, folding it up as he does so.* SONNY *rises and moves* L *of the bed*)

SONNY. Very nice. Very tasteful and nice.

ROSE. Do you remember those eyelashes? Those were from *Lido Lady*. Lily never threw anything away. And the eyeshadow's Meltonian Shoe Cream, because that's what Lady Lewisham uses. Meltonian Blue Suede.

IRIS. Well, we'd better hurry because Johnny'll be back soon with the people.

ROSE. What about a beauty spot?

SONNY. Now there's an idea. That *is* a nice idea, Rosie.

ROSE. There's that little crescent moon she wore in *The Countess Mitzi*.

SONNY. On the cheek, Rosie dear, just below the bone, and put a little glitter on it.

(JOHNNY *opens the door from outside to bring in* MADGE *and* MISS PEEL. MADGE *is dressed in a glamourized nurse's uniform and carries a briefcase.* MISS PEEL *is a temporary secretary*)

JOHNNY (*in the corridor*) In here.
SONNY. It's them.
ROSE. But we're not ready.
IRIS. Jimmy, don't let them in.
ROSE. They're to wait till she's ready.

(JIMMY *goes to the door and halts the visitors in the corridor.* SONNY *moves to the chair down* L)

JIMMY. Lily's not ready.
JOHNNY. Oh . . . (*He looks at the two women with him*) Er . . .
MADGE. Lily?
JOHNNY. Miss Terralozzi. (*He corrects himself*) Mrs Sims.
MADGE. But surely that's who . . . ?
JIMMY. That's right. She's dead, but she's not ready.
JOHNNY (*opening the door to the room* R) If you'd like to wait in here —I'm sure she won't be long. (*He crosses the room to down* R *and plugs in the fire*)

(MADGE *follows her to* LC, MISS PEEL *up* C, JIMMY *hovers by the doorway*)

MADGE. I'm afraid I don't understand. Why isn't the—why isn't your wife ready?
JIMMY (*from the door*) They're making her up.
JOHNNY. They're making her up.
JIMMY. Iris says she's to look her best.
JOHNNY. She has to look her best.
MADGE. But, Mr Sims, *we* do all that. It's part of the service.
JIMMY. I'll call you when she's ready. (*He goes into the room* L *and sits on the pouffe*)
JOHNNY. Miss Terralozzi was an artiste. She didn't like the public to see her unless she was looking her best.
MISS PEEL. There's a girl where I live does underwater ballet at the Victoria Palace. She looks a right slut in the daytime, but she doesn't care who sees her.
JOHNNY. Yes. It wasn't like that in our time. Miss Terralozzi had very high professional standards. (*Moving* L) Excuse me. I'm afraid the fire gives very little heat. It would be better not to remove your coats. (*He goes into the other room and moves* R *of the bed*)
MISS PEEL. Well! (*She sits on the bed*)
JOHNNY. Will you be long?
SONNY. We've done her neck and a beauty spot, dear. Now Iris'll do her hair.

JIMMY. What are they going to do, Johnny?

JOHNNY. They just want to have a look at her. Then I sign the papers, and get the money. Then they send a van to take her away.

IRIS. Well, they'll have to wait until she's ready.

(*They complete Lily's make-up during the following*)

MISS PEEL (*to Madge*) It's creepy, your job, do you know that? It's a real creep.

MADGE (*sitting on the bed, opening her briefcase and sorting papers*) No, it's clinical.

MISS PEEL. What's the difference?

MADGE. The future's in embalming. It's the modern way.

MISS PEEL. I do shorthand and typing and answer the telephone: that's what I'm trained for, not to collect bodies. (*She goes to the fire and warms her feet*)

MADGE. You don't have to collect anything. Just witness identification and the signature of next of kin. We have an arrangement with Carter Patterson for collection. They give the vanmen black armbands, and charge extra.

(LILY *now looks as if she were fully made up to make an appearance on the stage*)

JOHNNY. I'd better go back in.

IRIS. I won't be long. We'll send Jimmy in when she's ready.

JOHNNY. Yes. You've done very—she looks . . .

SONNY. She's the beautiful one, dear. She always was. And that dress was made for her.

JOHNNY. I'll go in. (*He moves* R)

SONNY. That dress was good enough for the Duke of Windsor, dear, so it ought to be good enough for God Almighty.

(JOHNNY *crosses from one room to the other*)

MISS PEEL. You can earn more money as a temporary secretary. And I could never settle to anything. Seeing the same boring people, day after day. I mean, you've got to live.

JOHNNY (*entering the* R *room*) She's nearly ready.

(SONNY *sits down* L)

MISS PEEL. You ought to have two bars on this fire.

JOHNNY. We try to economize.

MADGE (*moving to Johnny quickly, to distract*) I've got the papers here, Mr Sims, if you'd like to look at them. It's a very simple form of contract. (*She points to the place*) You see? "In consideration . . ."

(JOHNNY *sits down* L. MADGE *shows him the papers as she reads*)

"For purposes of demonstration only to bona fide students"—that's your guarantee against misuse.

JOHNNY (*looking*) Bona . . . fide . . .

MADGE. "All student work to be under fully qualified supervision"—that's Mr Knight junior—Mr Lloyd Knight: he's got degrees in it from the Ohio State University.

JOHNNY. Yes.

MADGE. "To be prepared for internment in a first-class manner.

JOHNNY. Internment?

MADGE. The funeral. First we leave a day for the lying-in-state, during which the near and dear may view and take their leave. Flowers are provided—whatever's seasonable and suitable—and there's continuous music of a reverential nature from a concealed source.

MISS PEEL. Frank Sinatra Sings Songs for Swinging Corpses.

MADGE. Please be quiet, Miss Peel, or I shall complain to the agency. (*To Johnny*) The funeral is by arrangement with the Bethesda Chapel down the road, unless special denominational facilities are requested. And Mr Lloyd Knight has bought a plot in the Walham Green Cemetery with the eventual intention of turning it into a Garden of Rest.

(JIMMY *rises, opens the door of the* L *room and calls*)

JIMMY. Ready now. (*He crosses the corridor*)

JOHNNY. Where do I sign?

MADGE. Down here. Your full name, please.

JIMMY. They've sent me. Lily's ready.

JOHNNY. I'm just signing the paper.

JIMMY. I'll tell them. (*He returns to the main room*)

JOHNNY. I haven't got a pen.

MADGE. Miss Peel, please get the presentation Gold Shaeffer from the briefcase.

MISS PEEL. The what?

MADGE. The pen!

(MISS PEEL *gets the pen and gives it to* MADGE, *who passes it on to Johnny*)

ROSE. Does he want us?

SONNY. We'd better watch, dear. It's an important moment. Then we can bring them in to see her.

(*They all move into the room* R. JOHNNY *is seated down* L, MADGE *stands* L *of him.* SONNY *stands above Johnny,* IRIS R *of Sonny and* ROSE R *of Iris.* JIMMY *creeps in between Iris and Rose.* MISS PEEL *watches from down* R)

JOHNNY. I'm going to sign with a gold pen.

JIMMY. When do we get the money?

MADGE. I have the cheque here.

JOHNNY. Cheque!

MADGE (*handing Johnny a cheque*)   Made out to cash, Mr Sims, as you requested.

Jimmy. There's not much time. You've got to do the shopping, and Iris'll cook.

Madge. Over the stamp, please.

Johnny. All my names?

Madge. Yes, please.

Sonny. He's got six, dear. Johnny's got six names.

Rose. John Raymond——

Jimmy. —Howard Godolphin——

Iris. —Destrange Sims.

Sonny. I hope there's room.

Johnny (*writing*) John—Raymond——

Madge. I've been telling Mr Sims that Miss—his wife—will lie in state for twenty-four hours. We have a special stateroom.

Miss Peel. With seasonal flowers and reverential music.

Johnny (*writing*) —Howard—Godolphin——

Madge. I'm sure you'll be most pleased and impressed when you see her.

Sonny. Oh, we shan't see her, dear. We don't go out.

Johnny (*writing*) —Destrange.

Iris. Mr Sims will go. We don't go out.

Johnny. What?

Rose. Iris was just telling the people. We don't go out. You go out.

Johnny. But you'll go to see Lil lying in state?

(*There is a pause. Everyone feels uncomfortable*)

Sonny. We never go out, Johnny. You know that.

Johnny. You'll come to the funeral with me?

Jimmy (*to Miss Peel*) We've not been out for thirteen years. We don't go out at all, you see. Johnny goes out . . .

Rose. We used to go out, but we don't go out now.

Johnny. But Lily—when they've . . . (*He looks to Madge for words*)

Madge. Prepared her for internment in a first-class manner.

Johnny. When they've done that. When she's there in a lead-lined coffin——

Madge. —with padded silk interior, pink or blue, according to sex——

Johnny. —waiting for you to pay your last respects. You mean—you won't pay your respects?

(*There is a silence, and a shiftiness. The others move uneasily away from Johnny*)

You won't come to see Lil buried?

(*Another silence.* Johnny *stands up*)

You wanted me to decide for myself, Iris. I have. I'm not signing. (*He hands the contract to Madge*)

Madge. Mr Sims!

Johnny (*moving* C) There's John Raymond Howard Godolphin Destrange on that paper but there's no Sims, and without Sims, it's not legal.

Madge. No, it isn't.

Sonny (*moving down stage*) But, Johnny dear, they've brought the money.

Johnny. And *you* won't go out.

Sonny (*with an angry appeal*) We *can't* go out.

Johnny. And I won't sign. (*To Iris*) That's right, isn't it, Iris? For forty years, I've done what Lily wanted, what you all wanted. I was glad to do it. I played percussion, and looked after the business side, and went out every day in all weathers to find things in the Underground, and I've taken them to Mr Davis, and we've lived on them. I've never done anything for myself or wanted to, only for Lily and for you. I've never taken a decision for myself, not for my own sake, and you've reproached me for it, Iris. I'm taking one now. You tell me how much you loved Lily. Well, you can show me how much you loved her. You'll go to Lily's funeral, or I won't sign, and there'll be no money for an anniversary. (*To Jimmy*) No turkey. (*To Rose*) No champagne. (*To them all*) Lying-in-state with reverent music, I don't care about that, I'm not used to it; it can take care of itself. But you'll come with me to Lily's funeral, or I won't sign.

(*There is a long pause*)

Rose. I'll go, Johnnie.
Jimmy. I'll go. We'll both go.

(*There is a pause.* Sonny *looks at Iris*)

Sonny. Well, *I* don't mind going. I've always said we should go out more often.

Jimmy. Have you? Then we'll all go out. We'll make a habit of it.

(*They wait to hear from* Iris)

Iris (*after a pause*) I won't go out. (*She returns to the main room and moves down* L)

Johnny (*to the others*) Well?
Sonny. Come on.

(Sonny *leads* Jimmy *and* Rose *across to the other room*)

Miss Peel (*to Johnny*) My father was like you. That's why I left home.

Rose (*moving below the bed*) Iris!
Jimmy (*moving* C) Please, Iris!
Sonny. Iris dear, he won't sign without you go.
Iris. No.
Rose. But you started it. (*She moves up* R *of the bed*)

JIMMY. You put it into his mind.
SONNY. Johnny never used to be like this.
IRIS. Lily wouldn't go out, and nor will I.
SONNY. Shut the door, Jimmy dear.

(JIMMY, *surprised, does so, then sits down* R)

Iris, if Johnny leaves us, we'll *have* to go out. We mustn't make him angry, dear.

JOHNNY (*after a pause*) Excuse me. (*He leaves Madge and Miss Peel, crosses the corridor, and opens the door to the main room*) Shutting the door, are you? (*He closes the door behind him*)

SONNY. Just a little conference, Johnny dear. Just something we wanted to say to Iris.

(JOHNNY *goes to the bed and looks down at the body*)

JOHNNY. She looks beautiful, Rosie. They—(*with a jerk of the head*) —won't make her look so nice, with all their chemicals.

ROSE (*taking Johnny's arm*) Do you like the beauty spot?

JOHNNY. It's the one she wore in *The Countess Mitzi.*

SONNY (*timid*) Iris did her hair, Johnny. Lily always had lovely hair, but it needed a lot of attention.

JOHNNY. Yes. (*He moves below the bed to Iris*) Well, Iris? You wanted me to make my mind up, and now you don't like it when I have.

IRIS. I've made mine up too. I'll not be forced to go out.

JOHNNY. Will you do it for love?

IRIS. That's not the point.

JOHNNY. But perhaps you didn't really want me to make up my own mind, old girl. Perhaps you just wanted to take Lil's place, and tell me what to do.

IRIS. I can't take Lily's place. I'm not your wife.

SONNY (*quickly*) I'm not having the cold room, Johnny dear. Not with my kidneys.

JOHNNY (*over his shoulder*) You'll have this room, you and Iris. I'll have the cold room.

IRIS. Lily wouldn't go out. She'd never go.

JOHNNY. Lily's dead. (*He pauses*) And I'm asking you to come with me and see her buried.

(IRIS *takes his hands in hers. There is a moment of silence, then she goes to the door, opens it, and calls across the corridor*)

IRIS. You can come in now. Mr Sims will sign.

(SONNY *quickly arranges them in position from* LC *down stage, so that the visitors can view the body. They line up,* SONNY *down stage, then* ROSE, JIMMY, JOHNNY *and* IRIS, *facing up stage.* MADGE *and* MISS PEEL *cross the corridor*)

JOHNNY. There's Lily. She's looking her best.

(MADGE *enters and moves* R *of the bed.* MISS PEEL *looks in from the hall*)

MADGE. What a pretty dress!

The lights fade to BLACK-OUT *as—*

the CURTAIN *falls*

FURNITURE AND PROPERTY LIST

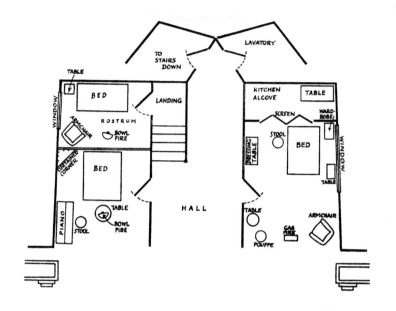

SCENE I

On stage: ROOM DOWN R:

Piano. *On it:* table lamp, sheet music

Piano stool. *In it:* music

Bed. *On it:* sheets, blanket, quilt, pillows. *Under it:* Sonny's slippers

Occasional table. *On it:* small electric fire, sequins, needle, cotton, blouse, *Readers' Digest*

Chair (down L)

On walls up R: hooks behind curtained corner. *On hook:* Sonny's overcoat

Worn rug

ROOM UP R:

Bed. *On it:* sheets, blanket, pillows, quilt

Small table (R) *On it:* table lamp

Chair (down R)

Worn rug

On floor down c: small electric fire
HALL:
Worn matting

ROOM L:
Occasional table (down R)
Pouffe
Dressing-table. *On it:* small hand-mirror, hairbrush. *In drawer:* paper, pencil, cigar-box with make-up, box of glitter and crescent-shaped beauty spot
Stool. *On it:* book
Bed. *On it:* sheets, blanket, bedspread, quilt, pillows
Large screen
Table (in kitchen alcove) *On it:* gas ring, tray with cups, beakers, glass of milk, milk jug, sugar. Tea ready in cups and beakers
Wardrobe (L) *In it:* large picture hat, coffee lace dress
Table (L) *On it:* table lamp
Gas fire
On back wall: large Underground map
Window curtains
Worn carpet

Off stage: Bundle of papers and magazines, including *The Lady* and *Evening Standard* (JOHNNY)
Packet of "Settlers" (JOHNNY)

Personal: DAVIS: watch
JOHNNY: Underground map

SCENE 2

Strike: Teacups and tray

Check: Sonny's slippers under bed and overcoat on hook

Set: Stool in L room to original position
Coffee lace dress concealed by bed in room L

Off stage: Briefcase with contract, cheque, gold Shaeffer pen, papers (MADGE)

LIGHTING PLOT

Property fittings required: 3 table lamps, 2 electric fires, gas fire
 A composite set
 THE APPARENT SOURCES OF LIGHT are: by day, windows in the "fourth wall"; by night, table lamps
 THE MAIN ACTING AREAS are down R, up RC, down RC, down C, LC, down L

SCENE I.. To open. Day. General dim lighting

Cue I	On CURTAIN up	(Page I)
	As ROSE, IRIS, *and* LILY *speak their first lines, bring up day lighting and fires in their respective rooms*	
Cue 2	IRIS switches off gas fire	(Page 6)
	Gas fire out	
Cue 3	SONNY turns on light	(Page 6)
	Snap on table lamp in room down R	
Cue 4	JIMMY turns off fire	(Page 8)
	Take out electric fire up R	
Cue 5	JOHNNY turns on light	(Page 9)
	Snap on table lamp in room L	
Cue 6	IRIS turns out light	(Page 12)
	Snap off lamp in room R	
Cue 7	JOHNNY turns on light	(Page 18)
	Snap on lamp in room R	
Cue 8	DAVIS: "It's the highest I can go"	(Page 22)
	Fade to Black-Out	

SCENE 2. To open. Night. Very dim general lighting

Cue 9	JOHNNY switches on light	(Page 23)
	Snap on lamp and lights in room L	
Cue 10	IRIS switches on light	(Page 24)
	Snap on lamp and lights in room down R	
Cue 11	JIMMY switches on light	(Page 24)
	Snap on lamp and lights in room up R	
Cue 12	IRIS lights gas fire	(Page 24)
	Bring up gas fire effect	
Cue 13	JIMMY turns off light	(Page 25)
	Snap off lamp and lights in room up R	

Cue 14	JOHNNY: ". . . she must look her best" *Fade to Black-Out*	(Page 30)
Cue 15	When ready *Fade up to previous lighting*	(Page 30)
Cue 16	JOHNNY plugs in fire *Brings on electric fire in room down* R	(Page 31)
Cue 17	MADGE: "What a pretty dress!" *Fade to Black-Out*	(Page 37)

EFFECTS PLOT

SCENE 1

Cue 1	LILY: "He must take great care" *Doorbell rings twice*	(Page 17)

SCENE 2

Cue 2	ROSE: "Don't lie on your back" *Noise of shunting train*	(Page 23)
Cue 3	JOHNNY switches on light *Lavatory flushes*	(Page 23)

TREVOR

SCENE—*The same set of rooms as we have already seen in " The Coffee Lace"
but this is Kensington, not Kennington. A Saturday afternoon in February.*
  *This is a flat (two rooms, kitchen and bathroom) shared by a couple of
young women in their late twenties, both earning a good salary. It has been
fairly recently decorated, and the furniture, pictures and objects have been
collected over the last three years, so that they express a unity of taste in a
pleasant "Sunday Colour Magazine" way. Books, record-player, television,
indirect lighting, central heating. Wall-to-wall carpets in the downstairs
room and the hall. There is a door-telephone set in the wall of the hall and
an ordinary telephone on a hall table. The small upstairs room has
become a Habitat kitchen. What was the door to a rather squalid W.C.
now opens to a well-furnished bathroom. There is one rather odd aspect of
the set which will not be immediately obvious, but will appear—what are
normally a bedroom and living-room have been hastily rearranged to look
like two bed-sitters.*
When the CURTAIN *rises,* JANE *is discovered lying on the divan in the* R
*room, smoking a cigarette and reading a book. On a coffee-table below the
divan is a tray containing tea-things. The door from outside is opened by a
latchkey.* JANE *looks up and listens.* SARAH *enters, bringing* TREVOR *into
the hall.*

SARAH. Shall I take your coat?
TREVOR (*in a slight northern accent*) What? Yes. Thank you.

  (SARAH *hangs up his coat together with her own, which she removes
without his help, on the hook on the hall wall,* L)

SARAH. Straight in. It's the door on the left.

  (TREVOR *goes into the room stage* L. *He looks around, admiring the
room, and clearly a stranger to it. Having hung up the coats,* SARAH
follows, closing the door behind her)

TREVOR (*moving* C *below the divan*) You've got a nice place here.
SARAH. I share it with another girl.
TREVOR. You've each got your own room?
SARAH (*moving above the armchair down* R) Yes, and we share the
kitchen and bathroom.
TREVOR. Where is she? (*He moves round the divan to up* L)
SARAH. She's gone out.

D

(JANE *looks at her watch. Then she returns to reading.* TREVOR *unconsciously picks up a bottle from the drinks table*)

Would you like a drink?

TREVOR. I'm not used to this.

SARAH. To what?

TREVOR (*returning* C) This—(*with a gesture*)—luxury.

SARAH. Oh, really!

TREVOR. And I'm not used to being taken home by girls as a matter of fact.

SARAH. Who usually takes you home?

TREVOR. That's not what I meant. Of course—my own place . . .

SARAH. Yes?

TREVOR. It's not much to take anyone back to.

SARAH. Why not?

TREVOR. I haven't got much money.

SARAH. Then why fritter it away, hanging around pubs?

TREVOR. You've got to do something.

SARAH. You could try work.

TREVOR. I told you; I'm an actor.

SARAH. Sorry. I forgot.

TREVOR. What do *you* do?

SARAH. I told you; I design fabrics.

TREVOR. That's right; you did. (*He sits on the divan*) Shall we—I mean, do you want to sit down?

SARAH (*sits in the chair down* R) Thank you.

(TREVOR *rises, moves* R *and hovers, uncertain whether he is expected to share the chair with her*)

TREVOR. Shall I sit down with you?

SARAH. No.

(*There is a pause.* JANE *looks up, looks at her watch again, half gets up, decides against it, and returns to reading*)

TREVOR. You're a funny girl.

SARAH. Why?

TREVOR. I mean, you picked *me* up. Standing there in your plastic mac, rubbing yourself up against me.

SARAH. I was not rubbing . . .

TREVOR. Asking me to come home with you.

SARAH. For a drink.

TREVOR. I thought you wanted to make all the running. Well, I didn't mind. Only now it looks as if I've got to do it. I'm not very good at that, as a matter of fact, because I'm a bit shy. I've got no instinct for it. I never know when it's time to put my hand on your leg—I mean, what the right moment is. Every girl I've ever been with has had to—sort of let me know—you know, tactfully. They move—(*he moves slightly towards Sarah*)—tactfully. I always have to know it's all right before I can go on to the next step.

SARAH (*rising*) I'll get you that drink. (*She goes to the drinks table*)

TREVOR. Don't bother. I'm not much good if I've had too much to drink, as a matter of fact.

SARAH. There's vodka and tonic.

TREVOR (*sitting in the chair down* R) Thank you.

(JANE *looks at her watch again, gets up, opens her door cautiously, goes into the hall, and on up to the kitchen. She starts to roll out dough which is prepared, and cutting scones. She puts them on a baking tray in the oven.* SARAH *gives Trevor his drink.* TREVOR *thanks her.* SARAH *goes to sit on the divan.* JANE *puts the rolling-pin down heavily on the kitchen table.* TREVOR *hears this*)

What was that?

SARAH. What?

TREVOR. I thought I heard something.

SARAH. It's an old house. It makes noises.

TREVOR. Oh.

SARAH. Built by Gianino Pisco in eighteen-twenty-four. You'll find it in *The A to Z of Historic London* if you're interested. Under P.

TREVOR. Ah.

(*There is a pause*)

SARAH ⎱ (*together*) ⎰ Do you . . .
TREVOR ⎰   ⎱ *You* aren't . . .

SARAH. I'm sorry.

TREVOR. *You* aren't having a drink.

SARAH. No. I had more than I wanted in the pub.

(*There is a pause, then* JANE *makes another noise in the kitchen.* TREVOR *looks up, but* SARAH *appears not to have noticed.* TREVOR *rises, puts his drink on the coffee-table below the divan, and goes towards* SARAH. *She rises instantly*)

Don't *touch* me! (*She moves below the armchair down* R)

TREVOR. What?

SARAH. I don't want you to touch me.

TREVOR. I'm sorry.

SARAH. No, it's my fault. I'm sorry, Trevor. I'm very nervous.

TREVOR. My name's not Trevor.

SARAH. Never mind.

TREVOR. Why did you think I was called Trevor?

SARAH. It doesn't matter.

TREVOR. Did you go to that pub to meet someone called Trevor? Have you made a mistake?

SARAH. I did, and I haven't.

TREVOR. What?

SARAH. I did go to that pub to meet someone called Trevor, and I haven't made a mistake.

TREVOR. I don't understand you.

SARAH (*noticing his slight accent*) You're from the north, aren't you? You're what they call a new wave actor.

TREVOR. Yes. There's a lot of us. That's why I'm not in work.

SARAH. Please sit down. Finish your drink. (*She hands it to him*) I'm sorry I snapped at you. (*She moves above the divan to* C)

(TREVOR *goes back to his chair.* JANE *puts the scones into the oven. Then she looks at her watch again, and comes back into the hall*)

TREVOR. I wish I knew what you're talking about.

(JANE *hesitates, then enters the room* L)

JANE. Well?

SARAH. Trevor, this is Jane.

(TREVOR *rises*)

JANE. Have you told him? (*She moves above the divan to Sarah*)

SARAH. Not yet.

(TREVOR *sits*)

JANE. It's three-forty-five. I've just put the scones in.

TREVOR. Er . . . (*He crosses his legs*)

JANE. There's only half an hour.

SARAH. How long do they take? The scones?

JANE. Don't worry about it. I'll see to it.

SARAH. Is there anything you want me to do?

JANE. No. I did it all while you were out.

(TREVOR *crosses his legs the other way. They look at him, considering how to start.* JANE *begins*)

Trevor . . .

TREVOR. I'm sorry. I told your friend. My name's not Trevor.

JANE. Yes, it is.

TREVOR. She made a mistake.

SARAH (*to Jane*) He was on his own. (*Moving down* L *of the divan*) He's an out-of-work actor. He needs money. I'm sorry about the accent, but a lot of people have accents now, you know they do.

JANE. The accent doesn't matter. If they take against him, they'll be all the more pleased when I break it off.

TREVOR. Look . . . (*He recrosses his legs uncomfortably*)

JANE. Don't worry. We're just going to explain.

TREVOR. Then, if you wouldn't mind . . .

SARAH (*moving below the divan*) Yes?

TREVOR. I mean, if it's going to take a bit of time . . .

JANE (*looking at her watch*) It can't take much.

TREVOR. I had a lot of beer in that pub, and . . .

SARAH (*moving* R *and opening the door*) It's at the end of the hall.

TREVOR (*rising*) Thank you. (*He puts the drink on the coffee-table, leaves the room and goes up the hall*)

JANE. You took your time.
SARAH (*closing the door*) It wasn't easy.

(TREVOR *exits into the bathroom*)

JANE. All you had to do was go up to someone and . . .
SARAH. You can't just approach a man like that. I had to stand there for hours, rubbing myself up against him.
JANE. Rubbing yourself up!
SARAH. Metaphorically. Then when we got back, he thought . . .
JANE. I know what he thought.
SARAH (*moving to the table down* R *and lighting a cigarette*) Well, he was bound to. I had to discourage him.
JANE (*moving to Sarah*) Love, I'm sorry. I am sorry, love. I was here—reading—wondering.
SARAH. I know. I could feel you wondering all the way from the pub. Wonder and jealousy. It was very thick on the stairs when we came in.
JANE. Jealous! Of him?
SARAH. You'd be jealous of the *Manchester Guardian* if it was delivered every day.
JANE. I'll tell him. I'll just put it to him. He can only say, No.
SARAH (*sitting in the armchair down* R) I wish we didn't have to.
JANE. We do have to.
SARAH. Couldn't we say Trevor had a business conference or something?
JANE. Script conference. My Trevor writes for television: do try to remember. *Your* Trevor's in I.C.I. (*She moves above the divan*)
SARAH. Sorry. Couldn't we say he had a script conference, and couldn't get here? Then I'd ring up from a phone-box, and pretend to be him.

(JANE *gives her a look*)

Well, they wouldn't hear my end of the conversation.

(*The W.C. is flushed in the bathroom.* TREVOR *appears and comes down the hall*)

JANE. We'll have to do that anyway if he refuses.

(TREVOR *enters the* L *room*)

TREVOR (*moving* R *of the divan*) Who uses Arpège? I took some. I like using other people's things: it's a kind of kleptomania. I thought I might brush my teeth with your toothbrush, but I don't really know you well enough, do I?
SARAH. I can smell the Arpège. It's very strong.
TREVOR (*crossing* L *below the divan*) That's the trouble. When it belongs to somebody else, I always put too much on.
JANE (*moving to him*) Trevor . . .
TREVOR. I told you . . .

JANE. That's the first thing. You've got to get used to answering to the name.

TREVOR. Why?

JANE. Just listen. You're not very well off, are you?

TREVOR. No. (*He sits down* L)

JANE. And you're an actor.

TREVOR. Yes.

JANE. We want you to act.

TREVOR. What in?

JANE. Just for this afternoon. (*She sits on the divan*) My parents are coming to tea. They live in Paignton, and I hardly ever see them, but once a year they make a family tour—a week-end in Maidenhead with my married sister, during which they visit me, then up to Buxton to my brother . . .

SARAH. He's a mining engineer. You might have met him.

TREVOR. I'm from Bolton.

SARAH. It's all the north, isn't it?

JANE. Then back home. They'll be here in (*looking at her watch*) fifteen minutes. They must think you're my fiancé.

TREVOR. Where is your fiancé?

JANE. I haven't got a fiancé. But I'm twenty-seven. My parents think I should have one.

TREVOR (*to Sarah*) But why did *you* . . .

SARAH. I picked you up because Jane's a friend of mine. She had to get things ready here. Finding you was the best way to help her.

TREVOR (*to Jane*) But twenty-seven's nothing. People get engaged at any age.

JANE. That's what I tell my parents. But my mother is rather a bossy woman, Trevor. She doesn't want me to become a dried-up spinster, and she does want to see some positive evidence of my intention to avoid that. (*She pauses*) But don't worry. I shall certainly break it off. It won't come to anything.

SARAH. We thought if you played up your accent a bit, and took milk first in tea, and dribbled your scones, Jane's mother might break it off herself.

TREVOR. But why couldn't you get one of your own friends to do it?

JANE. We'll pay you five pounds for the afternoon. Do you agree?

TREVOR (*after a pause*) I see. (*He rises and moves his chair*)

JANE. What do you see?

TREVOR. If this is a bed-sitter, where's the dressing-table?

JANE. In the other room.

TREVOR. The bedroom?

JANE. Yes. (*To Sarah*) He's quick, isn't he? It must come from working in the theatre.

TREVOR (*moving* C; *to Sarah*) And *your* mother?

SARAH (*rising*) My mother's the President of the local Liberal

Party, and she runs the Welfare Clinic, and she does part-time teaching of retarded children. She doesn't care if I get married or not, but she says she'd like me to be sexually fulfilled. Consequently *my* Trevor is a married man who works for Shell.

JANE (*rising and standing between them*) I.C.I.

SARAH (*putting out her cigarette*) I.C.I. (*To Trevor*) But you don't have to bother about *my* Trevor.

TREVOR. What a pity!

SARAH. Do you need work that badly?

TREVOR. I didn't mean that. I meant—what a pity! I'm sorry.

JANE. We don't need your pity. Will you take the job?

(*The door buzzer sounds*)

(*Looking at her watch*) They're early. Quickly—will you do it?

TREVOR. Yes.

JANE (*going*) Sarah, fill him in. (*She goes to answer the door by the door-phone*)

(SARAH *hastily briefs* TREVOR, *drowning* JANE *at the door-phone*)

SARAH. You're Trevor Hudson. You live in Chelsea—quite near here—in Paultons Square—a flat. Christ, I can't remember the number. Never mind; they won't ask. You're a staff-writer for the B.B.C.: that's why you never get your name in the *Radio Times*. You do research and linking bits for programmes about animals and the Common Market. (*Moving down* R) You're writing a novel. It takes you ages because you can never think of the right words. You had some poems published when you were at the university.

JANE. Mother? . . . What? . . . I can't hear . . . Oh! . . . Yes . . . I'm sorry; the door buzzer isn't working. She'll have to come down.

TREVOR (*following Sarah down* R) Which?

SARAH. Any you like.

(JANE *moves from the door-phone*)

TREVOR. Oxford, then. I did *Charley's Aunt* at Southport two years ago.

(JANE *returns to the room* L, *appalled*)

JANE (*moving* C) It's *your* parents.

SARAH. What?

JANE. It's your parents. They wanted to surprise you. I told them the buzzer wasn't working. You'll have to go down and let them in.

SARAH. Jesus! (*Going quickly*) Fill him in.

(SARAH *runs out by the hall door*)

JANE. Trevor works for I.C.I. He's married.

TREVOR. What about the scones? Shouldn't we take them out of the oven?

JANE (*looking at her watch*) Oh God! God! Come on!

(TREVOR *follows* JANE *quickly upstairs to the kitchen to get the scones out of the oven*)

Trevor has two children. Twins. They were an accident. He doesn't like them much.

TREVOR. What's his name?

JANE. Hudson.

TREVOR. But that's . . .

JANE (*taking the scones out of the oven and putting them on the table*) They're both called Hudson. Both Trevors. Hers and mine.

TREVOR (*finding an apron behind the door and putting it on*) Convenient.

JANE. It's the landlord's name.

TREVOR. Trevor?

JANE. Hudson. Trevor, do listen! Trevor's an economist. He . . .

TREVOR. What's the landlord's first name?

JANE. How do *I* know? Landlords don't have first names. Put the scones in that basket, and cover them with a napkin. I'd better make some more.

TREVOR (*following her instructions*) He's an economist?

JANE. Very brilliant and young. (*She picks up a kettle from the sink*) He was married at eighteen. That's where the twins came from. It was a shotgun wedding in the chapel at Dulwich College. He and Sarah met at the National Gallery one lunch-time. He picked her up in front of a Study of Small Children Being Mobbed by Apes.

TREVOR. He did?

JANE. No. *I* did.

(*The door outside opens and* SARAH's *voice is heard.* JANE *and* TREVOR *react*)

SARAH. Go straight in.

(MR *and* MRS LAWRENCE *enter.* SARAH *follows*)

I'll take your coat, Mother. (*She hangs up Mrs Lawrence's coat*) It's the room on the left.

(MR LAWRENCE *hands Sarah his coat*)

TREVOR. There they are.

JANE. You'd better take the scones down.

(SARAH *hangs up Mr Lawrence's coat*)

MRS LAWRENCE. I thought you said Trevor was here.

SARAH. He is.

(MRS LAWRENCE *goes into Sarah's room*)

MRS LAWRENCE. No, he isn't.
TREVOR (*to Jane*) Hey!
JANE. Yes?
TREVOR. What do I do when *your* parents come?

(MR LAWRENCE *takes cigars and matches from his overcoat*)

JANE. I'll have to tell them Trevor had a script conference.
TREVOR. I could drop in for a drink later.
JANE. *You* could?
TREVOR. Trevor could.
MRS LAWRENCE. He's not here, Sarah.

(SARAH *joins Mr Lawrence in the room*)

SARAH. Well, he should be. (*Calling from the door*) Trevor!
TREVOR (*calling*) I'm in the kitchen, making some scones. (*He comes downstairs, carrying the scones in a basket, with a napkin over them*)

(JANE *puts the kettle on and lays a tray for tea, but forgets the cups. In the hall,* TREVOR *stops to speak to Mr Lawrence*)

How do you do?

(MRS LAWRENCE *sits on the divan.* SARAH *hovers*)

MR LAWRENCE. Very well, thank you.
TREVOR. Stock market's recovering, I see.
MR LAWRENCE. What?
TREVOR. Stocks and shares. They're very buoyant.
MR LAWRENCE. Oh. Good.
TREVOR. You have to keep a sharp eye on the state of the market in my job. I'll take these in. (*He goes into Sarah's room with the scones*)

(MR LAWRENCE *has begun to get the full aroma of the Arpège. He gazes after Trevor, and sniffs the air, surprised, then follows him in*)

Scones. Eat them while they're hot.
SARAH. Mother, this is Trevor.
TREVOR. How do you do? Your husband and I have just been discussing stocks and shares.
MRS LAWRENCE. I'm so glad to meet you, Trevor. I've heard a lot about you. (*To Sarah*) Sarah dear, you're wearing a very heavy perfume. I didn't notice it when we came in.
TREVOR. No, it's me. I put too much on. (*With a sudden thought*) Oh, my Gawd, I forgot the kettle. (*He gives Sarah the scones and hurries out of the room and up to the kitchen*)

(MR *and* MRS LAWRENCE *look after him, and then at each other*)

MRS LAWRENCE. *That's* Trevor?
SARAH. I told you so, Mother.
MRS LAWRENCE. My dear, I hope you haven't made a mistake.
SARAH. Don't be ridiculous. (*She puts the scones on the table* C)

Mr Lawrence (*moving slowly above the divan to up* L) What was that about stocks and shares? (*He lights a cigar*)

Sarah (*moving* L *of the divan*) He takes an interest in them. (*She sits* L *on the divan*)

(Trevor *reaches the kitchen and sees the kettle already on*)

Trevor. Oh, you've done it. What about the cups and saucers?

Jane. There's the tray. How's it going?

Trevor. Early to say. I'm concentrating on making a good impression. No cake?

Jane. There's a cake in the other room. You'd better cut it in half.

(Trevor *gathers up the tray*)

Trevor. I'll come back when it whistles.

Jane. No. Let Sarah do it.

Trevor. Oh, I don't . . . (*Realizing Jane needs reassurance*) Righty-ho. (*Ready to go downstairs*) I'd start making those extra scones if I were you. Cups. (*He takes five cups from the shelves and arranges them on the tray*)

(Jane *takes a packet of Scone Mix from the cupboard and begins on the scones*)

Mrs Lawrence. Now we *are* here, we can take you and Trevor out for the evening. Your father's brought his Barclaycard.

(Mr Lawrence *reacts*)

Sarah. But Trevor's married. He has a family in Blackheath.

Mrs Lawrence. Then what's he doing here, baking scones?

Sarah. He comes round on Saturday afternoons sometimes.

Mrs Lawrence. Don't be silly, Sarah. If you only had the afternoon, you'd spend it in bed, not up to your elbows in dough.

Mr Lawrence. Steady on, Hetty.

Sarah. As a matter of fact, we . . .

(Trevor *leaves the kitchen with the tray*)

Mrs Lawrence. Don't say you've been. That bed's not even rumpled.

Mr Lawrence. Hetty!

Mrs Lawrence. I've no time for prudery about sex, Harold. You ought to know that, if anyone does.

Mr Lawrence. I do, dear; I do.

(Trevor *comes into the room* L)

Mrs Lawrence. Trevor, my husband and I thought you and Sarah might like to come out with us this evening. There was a Hungarian film in the Sunday papers.

Trevor. Hungarian? (*He puts the tray on the table down* R)

SARAH. I'll help you.

(TREVOR *and* SARAH *arrange the teacups*)

MRS LAWRENCE. We hardly ever see Hungarian films in Bury St Edmunds. If one has to come to London, one oughtn't to waste the trip. (*To Sarah*) I've already taken your father round the Victoria and Albert Museum.

MR LAWRENCE (*picking up an ashtray from the drinks table and sitting* L *on the divan*) I'll sit down for a bit if I may, and take my shoes off.

(MRS LAWRENCE *looks disapproving.* MR LAWRENCE *rises and sits in the chair down* L)

We'll see the six o'clock show, and have dinner afterwards. Then we'll be able to catch the ten-forty-five home. Harold, what did you do with the Good Food Guide?

MR LAWRENCE (*indicating her handbag*) It's in there.

MRS LAWRENCE. We'd better find somewhere to eat between King's Cross and the Curzon Cinema.

TREVOR. That'll be lovely.

SARAH. But Kathy's expecting you. (*With a slight emphasis*) At home.

(MR LAWRENCE *starts to take his shoes off*)

TREVOR. Who? Oh, Kathy. Yes, that's right; Kathy's expecting me. (*To Mrs Lawrence*) I've got a wife and family. (*To Mr Lawrence*) Twins. But I don't like them very much. If it hadn't been for them, I wouldn't be married. It's hard to forgive a thing like that.

SARAH. You're not trying, are you?

TREVOR. I'd better get the cake. (*To Mrs Lawrence*) We're only having half a cake because Jane's expecting *her* parents.

(*The buzzer sounds.* JANE *hears it and begins to come downstairs, leaving the scones on the baking tray*)

That's them now. (*He goes out of the room and meets Jane in the hall*) Getting the cake.

JANE. I haven't had time to put the scones in.

(TREVOR *goes into the* R *room.* JANE *answers the door-phone. The following speeches overlap*)

MRS LAWRENCE. Jane? That's the girl?	JANE. Mother? Do come up. Push the door when it buzzes.
SARAH. The girl I share with.	

MR LAWRENCE (*with his shoes off*) That's better. That's much better.

(JANE *pushes the buzzer that lets people in downstairs.* TREVOR *fusses with cutting the cake in half and looking for another plate to put his half* on. *He finds one under a pot plant on the shelves* R, *wipes it on his trousers and puts the cake on it*)

MRS LAWRENCE. How do you get on with her? You never say.

(JANE *opens the outer door and looks downstairs*)

SARAH. Oh, very well. We don't really see much of each other. She has her friends, and I have mine. She's engaged, as a matter of fact.

(*The kettle whistles*)

TREVOR (*moving to the door and shouting*) Sarah, can you go?
SARAH. I won't be a moment, Mother. (*She goes into the hall*)

(JANE *turns to her for a moment.* SARAH *takes Jane's hand, and squeezes it, then goes quickly up into the kitchen.* JANE *turns to look after her*)

MRS LAWRENCE. There's something wrong with that young man.
MR LAWRENCE. Lots of men wear scent nowadays.
MRS LAWRENCE. If one's going to be somebody's mistress, it's not up to *him* to bake the scones. It's not the basis of a satisfactory relationship. I think we'd better find out a little more about him.

(JANE'S *attention is still on the stairs where Sarah went.* MRS KEMPTON *comes sailing in through the outer door*)

MRS KEMPTON. Jane, dear!
JANE. Hullo, Mother.

(MRS KEMPTON *folds Jane in her arms as* TREVOR *comes out of the room* R *with half a cake inadequately put out on the plate.* MRS KEMPTON *drops Jane and advances to him*)

MRS KEMPTON. And you're Trevor.
TREVOR. Yes.
JANE. No! (*She moves behind her mother to sign to Trevor*)
TREVOR. Eh?

(MRS KEMPTON *sniffs and turns to Jane*)

MRS KEMPTON. Jane, you're wearing too much perfume.
TREVOR. No, it's me.
MRS KEMPTON. I beg your pardon.
TREVOR. I went a bit mad with the Arpège. Nerves, I expect. Knowing I was going to meet you.
JANE. Mother, you've made a mistake.
MRS KEMPTON. No, no, Jane dear, it's quite all right. (*To Trevor*) I understand.
JANE. No, you don't.
MRS KEMPTON. Trevor wished to make a good impression on his fiancée's parents, and accidentally put on too much after-shaving lotion. That's not hard to understand.

(MR KEMPTON *enters, exhausted by the stairs*)

Harold, this is Trevor.

JANE. No, it isn't.

MRS KEMPTON (*to Trevor*) My husband takes longer to come up-stairs than I because he likes to have a little rest on every landing.

TREVOR. How do you do, Mr . . . er . . .

MR KEMPTON. How do! She ought to have a lift. You tell her. (*To Jane*) You ought to have a lift, Janey. Get one put in. (*He kisses Jane, hangs up his coat, then sits on the stool down L in the hall*)

JANE. Mother, this isn't Trevor.

MRS KEMPTON. What?

JANE. This isn't Trevor.

MRS KEMPTON. But . . .

TREVOR. Well—maybe I'm not.

MRS KEMPTON. Then why did you say you were?

(SARAH *appears from the kitchen with the teapot*)

SARAH. Trevor . . .

(*They all look at* SARAH, *who stops dead*)

MRS KEMPTON. I don't know what's got into you, Jane.

SARAH. I'm so sorry. I interrupted.

MRS KEMPTON (*to Trevor*) Are you Trevor or are you not?

TREVOR. Sort of Yes and No, in a manner of speaking.

JANE. Mother . . .

MRS KEMPTON. Just a minute, Jane. (*To Sarah*) You're the girl my daughter shares the flat with. How do you do?

SARAH. Yes, I am. (*She comes half-way downstairs*) How do you do?

MRS KEMPTON. Sarah Lawrence.

SARAH. Yes. You're Mrs Kempton.

MRS KEMPTON. Exactly. (*She indicates Mr Kempton*) My husband.

MR KEMPTON. How do you do?

MRS KEMPTON. I know your name, Miss Lawrence. Little else. Jane writes very little about you.

SARAH. I'm sorry.

MRS KEMPTON. Don't apologize. You have your own life to lead; that's as it should be. Sharing a flat is a matter of convenience. I don't approve of close friendships between young women.

TREVOR. I'll just take the cake in. (*He moves a step towards the room L*)

MRS KEMPTON (*to Sarah*) You know Mr Hudson, of course?

SARAH. Trevor? Yes. (*She comes to the foot of the stairs*)

MRS KEMPTON. Thank you. (*To Trevor*) Take the cake in, Trevor, by all means. I shall join you in a moment. Jane dear, no doubt you wish to show me where to wash my hands. Harold, follow Trevor.

TREVOR (*giving Sarah the cake*) It's yours.

JANE (*indicating the bathroom door*) In here, Mother.

(SARAH *forestalls surprise in Mrs Kempton*)

SARAH. My parents have come to tea unexpectedly. Trevor thought I ought to have half the cake.

MRS KEMPTON. Ah! I am glad my daughter bought one large enough.

JANE. This *way*, Mother.

(MRS KEMPTON *and* JANE *go into the bathroom.* SARAH *and* TREVOR *look at Mr Kempton*)

SARAH. Will you be coming in to say hullo to my parents?

TREVOR. I think I'd better, don't you?

SARAH. I'm sure you'd better.

TREVOR (*to Mr Kempton*) Sarah's father's very interested in writing for television. We don't often get the chance to talk.

MR KEMPTON (*rising*) Which is Jane's room?

TREVOR (*pointing*) That one.

MR KEMPTON. I'll just take my shoes off. We've been to see Queen Mary's dolls. My wife likes to keep active. (*He goes into Jane's room, sits* R *on the divan and takes his shoes off*)

SARAH. What happened?

TREVOR. She thought I was Jane's Trevor.

SARAH. So I gather. And Jane?

TREVOR. Wanted *you* to have me.

SARAH. Yes. Blast! I mucked it up.

TREVOR. Now you've both got me.

SARAH. But hardly both at once.

TREVOR. It's just like *The Corsican Brothers* I must say. I've always wanted to play twins. I'd better come in with you for a bit, and then get back to the others.

SARAH (*giving the cake back to Trevor*) Take the cake.

(SARAH *opens the door* L *and enters her own room.* TREVOR *following*)

MRS LAWRENCE. Trevor . . .

(*At the same time the bathroom door opens and* MRS KEMPTON *comes out*)

MRS KEMPTON (*simultaneously*) Trevor . . .

(*A frozen moment. Then the phone rings*)

TREVOR (*quickly giving Sarah the cake*) I think it's for me. (*He answers the phone*) Hullo? . . . What? . . . This is Trevor Hudson speaking. Yes, it's I.

(TREVOR *signs secretly to* SARAH *who enters the room* L *and closes the door.* TREVOR *gives a conciliatory smile to Mrs Kempton. Then, unseen by her, but seen by the audience, cuts himself off from the caller at the other end, while continuing to speak*)

No, you tell Huw Wheldon I can't do it for that. He'll have to get Jonathan Miller. . . . No, I'm sorry. Not a penny under two thousand . . . That's right. You tell him. (*He puts down the phone and his smile to Mrs Kempton is much more confident*)

(JANE *comes from the bathroom*)

I'm so sorry. Do forgive me. It's really not at all important, but my agent gets distraught if he doesn't know where to find me. Do please go in. Jane, did you put the kettle on? (*He opens the door of Jane's room*)

JANE. No.

TREVOR. I'll do it. (*To Mrs Kempton, holding the door*) With you in a moment. I just want to whip up some scones to supplement the cake.

MRS KEMPTON. Whip?

TREVOR. Only a manner of speaking. Nothing kinky.

(MRS KEMPTON *enters the room, giving another sniff at the reek of Trevor's Arpège. MR KEMPTON looks up at her. TREVOR collapses against the banisters*)

MR KEMPTON. I thought I'd take my shoes off.

MRS KEMPTON. There's something odd about that young man.

MR KEMPTON. Oh, I don't know. Lots of men wear scent nowadays. I thought it was rather attractive.

MRS KEMPTON. That will do, Harold.

MR KEMPTON. He's a writer, isn't he? Bound to be artistic.

MRS KEMPTON. I don't want Jane getting into the newspapers. (*Sitting* L *on the divan*) I think we'd better find out a little more about him. Why isn't there a wardrobe in here?

JANE. Who was on the phone?

TREVOR. I don't know. Someone with asthma.

JANE. What?

TREVOR. Heavy breathing.

JANE. Oh—him.

TREVOR. You know him?

JANE. All the women in this district know him. He's called the Chelsea Breather. I usually put the phone down.

TREVOR. Well, let him breathe a bit next time. You owe him something. He saved my life. I'll get the scones in. That should give me a few minutes with Sarah's parents while they're baking. (*As he goes upstairs*) I hope you noticed that two thousand quid's my minimum fee for scripts.

(MR LAWRENCE *takes a scone and begins to eat*)

JANE. Yes. As far as my parents know, that's how much you make in a year. (*She moves to the room* R)

TREVOR. Ah! Well, you can't win them all.

(JANE *goes in to her parents and sits down* L. TREVOR *goes to the kitchen, and puts scones in the oven. He looks round for something to serve them on, and finds a plate and napkin*)

MRS LAWRENCE. Where's Trevor?

SARAH (*moving down* R) He had a phone call. Business. (*She pours two cups of tea*)

MRS LAWRENCE. He's gone?

SARAH. No. He'll be in in a minute.

MR KEMPTON. Where's Trevor?

MRS KEMPTON. He had a phone call. Something about two thousand pounds.

MR KEMPTON. Good God!

MRS KEMPTON. He refused it.

MR LAWRENCE (*biting his scone*) He makes a good scone.

SARAH. He enjoys cooking. (*She hands tea to Mr and Mrs Lawrence*)

MRS LAWRENCE (*looking at Mr Lawrence*) I suppose he doesn't get the opportunity at home.

SARAH. No, his wife does it all.

MRS LAWRENCE. Is that why he comes here?

SARAH (*passing a plate, butter and jam to Mr Lawrence*) No, he comes to see me. As you know. (*She sits down* R)

MRS KEMPTON. I suppose men's after-shaving lotion is designed to linger nowadays.

JANE. Why do you say that?

MRS KEMPTON. If Trevor shaved this morning, it's still rather strong.

JANE. It's not after-shave; it's scent. It belongs to Sarah. Trevor found it in the bathroom and put some on just before you arrived.

MRS KEMPTON. Did he?

JANE. He told you; he was nervous.

MRS KEMPTON. It's all right, dear: I said I understood. (*She looks around*) There's something odd about this room. I'll put my finger on it in a minute.

(TREVOR *looks at the scones in the oven and comes downstairs to join the Lawrences, going quietly past the Kemptons' door*)

TREVOR (*making an entrance* L) Everybody happy?

MRS LAWRENCE. What was your phone call?

TREVOR. Oh—financial matters.

MRS LAWRENCE. On Saturday afternoon?

TREVOR. Well, you know how it is.

MRS LAWRENCE. No, I don't.

MR LAWRENCE. I don't either.

SARAH. Trevor does a lot of free-lance work in his spare time.

TREVOR. That's right. I've got a wife and family to support.

SARAH. He's a consultant.

TREVOR. Yes.

SARAH. Firms consult him.

TREVOR. Always at it.

SARAH. He advises them.

TREVOR. They pay for my advice.

MRS LAWRENCE. He must be very brilliant.

TREVOR. Yes, I am.

MRS LAWRENCE. Tell me, Trevor, what exactly do you do at I.C.I.?

TREVOR (*after a pause*) I'm glad you asked that question. (*He takes out a notebook and pencil, sits R of Mrs Lawrence, and begins to draw diagrams*)

MRS KEMPTON (*to Jane*) Jane dear, how much do you really know about Trevor?

JANE. I've told you. He's a scriptwriter. He's . . .

MRS KEMPTON. We know what he does for a living; that's not the point.

JANE. What is the point?

MRS KEMPTON. How well do you really know him?

MR KEMPTON. Your mother's afraid he might be a nancy boy.

JANE. What?

MR KEMPTON. Homosexual. You know the sort of things. Exposing himself in public lavatories.

JANE. Why?

MR KEMPTON. Just because he wears scent and likes cooking. I told her everybody wears scent these days. She said she didn't want you getting into the papers.

JANE (*to Mrs Kempton*) You don't approve of my fiancé, Mother?

MRS KEMPTON. I never said that. I just don't want you to rush into things and be sorry afterwards.

JANE. But you told me I ought to get married.

MRS KEMPTON. To the right man. Yes.

JANE. I wish you'd make your mind up. Last time, you said that at my age I couldn't afford to be choosey.

MRS KEMPTON (*after a pause*) He's a long time with the scones, dear. Do you think you ought to go and——

JANE. —see what he's up to? Don't worry, Mother. He's hardly likely to be exposing himself in the kitchen.

TREVOR. And that's it, really.

MRS LAWRENCE. It doesn't seem very clear to me.

SARAH. Of course it is, Mother. It's quite clear.

MRS LAWRENCE. But *do* large commercial corporations work like that?

TREVOR. Of course they do. If you watched television as much as I do, you'd know they do.

MRS KEMPTON (*rising*) He shouldn't be doing the cooking. It's not a man's job. I'll help him. (*She moves to the door*)

JANE (*rising*) No.

MRS KEMPTON. It will give us the chance for a little talk. (*She opens the door*) Trevor . . .

JANE. Mother, I said, No. (*She takes Mrs Kempton's place at the door*) I won't have you making Trevor nervous.

MRS KEMPTON. Really, Jane, what . . .

E

JANE. Trevor gets nervous very easily. I'll go. (*She goes into the hall, closing the door firmly behind her*)

MRS KEMPTON (*sitting*) I don't like this, Harold. I don't care for it at all.

(JANE *goes to the kitchen*)

MRS LAWRENCE. Was that someone calling?

SARAH. No, I don't think so.

MRS LAWRENCE. Somebody wanted Trevor. I heard them distinctly.

SARAH. Jane's parents are here. I told you.

MRS LAWRENCE. But what should they want with Trevor?

(JANE *leaves the kitchen and comes downstairs*)

TREVOR. I give them advice sometimes. On financial matters.

JANE *comes into the hall and hovers outside the bathroom door*)

JANE. Trevor?

MRS LAWRENCE. There!

SARAH. That was Jane.

MRS LAWRENCE. But why should Jane . . .

SARAH. Mother, don't be so suspicious of everything.

MRS LAWRENCE. Suspicious? I don't know what you mean. What is there to be suspicious about?

TREVOR (*to Sarah*) Don't you have a cat called Trevor?

SARAH (*angrily*) No.

TREVOR. Just trying to be helpful.

(JANE *still undecided, looks at the door of Sarah's room, then smells the scones burning in the kitchen*)

JANE. Oh Christ! The scones! (*She dashes upstairs, takes out the scones, puts them on a plate and covers them with a napkin*)

MRS KEMPTON. What are they talking about up there? They're a very long time.

MR KEMPTON. Dammit, they're engaged.

MRS KEMPTON. He's supposed to be meeting us, not gossiping with Jane in the kitchen. Besides, I don't want Jane talking about me to that young man.

MR KEMPTON. She's obviously done that already. That's why he put on all that scent.

TREVOR (*rising*) I suppose I ought to say Hullo to Jane's parents. I mean, they might be a bit hurt if I ignored them.

(JANE *moves to the kitchen door*)

SARAH. They're very fond of Trevor.

MRS LAWRENCE. I thought you said you saw very little of Jane.

SARAH. I don't see much of her. Trevor just happens to get on with her parents. He collects people.

Trevor. I'm terribly good with older women. (*Moving to the door*) Do excuse me. I shan't be a moment.

(Trevor *crosses the hall, opens the door, and goes in to Mr and Mrs Kempton, just missing* Jane *as she comes downstairs with the scones on a plate*)

Trevor. Everybody happy?
Mrs Kempton. But where's Jane?
Trevor. Jane?
Mrs Kempton. She went to fetch you.
Trevor. Did she? That's right: she did. (*To Mrs Kempton*) Jane went to fetch me. (*He sits in the armchair down* L)
Mrs Kempton. Then where is she?
Trevor. She hasn't come back yet.

(Jane *hesitates, then knocks at the door* L *and enters. She is surprised not to see Trevor*)

Er . . .

(*There is a pause. They all look at her*)

Jane. I—er . . .
Mrs Lawrence. Are you looking for my daughter's lover?
Mr Lawrence. Hetty!
Jane. No. No. I . . . (*She holds out the scones*) I just brought you these.
Mrs Lawrence. But we have scones already.
Jane. These are hot. (*She piles them on the others*)
Mrs Kempton. And where are the scones?
Trevor. Scones?
Mrs Kempton. You went to "whip them up".
Trevor (*rising*) That's right. They're ready. (*He goes to the door*) I'll get them.
Mrs Kempton. Can't Jane bring them?
Trevor. Oh, she'll need a bit of help. My scones are terribly heavy. (*He goes quickly into the hall and up into the kitchen, sees Jane isn't there, goes to take the scones out of the oven and finds they are gone*)
Jane (*backing to the door*) Well—I'd better get back.

(Trevor *gets out flour, milk and eggs*)

Sarah. Thank you for the scones.
Jane. That's quite all right.
Mr Lawrence (*eating another*) They're very good.

(Trevor *starts haphazardly mixing his ingredients*)

Mrs Lawrence. I have a great deal of difficulty keeping my husband away from starchy foods.
Jane (*going*) I'm so glad to have met you, Mrs Lawrence.

Mrs Lawrence. You will find Trevor with your parents. He is giving them advice on financial matters.

(Jane *goes out, crosses the hall and enters her room. She is surprised not to find Trevor with her parents*)

Mrs Kempton. And where is Trevor?
Jane. Trevor?
Mr Kempton. He went to help you.
Jane. Oh—Trevor. He's making scones. (*She sits down* l)
Mrs Kempton. Again!
Jane. The first lot didn't take.

(*The phone rings.* Jane *and* Sarah *both respond to it as a welcome diversion*)

Jane (*rising*) I'll go.
Sarah (*rising*) I'll go.

(Jane *and* Sarah *go to the hall.* Trevor *also hurries downstairs. They look at one another.* Jane *and* Sarah *shut their respective doors.* Trevor *picks up the receiver, holds it a moment, then replaces it*)

Trevor. Well? (*He sits on the stool*)
Sarah. I can't keep it up.
Trevor. *You* can't?
Sarah. We should never have started. It's ridiculous. Like a farce.
Jane. We can't tell them.
Sarah. I'm sick of it. I'm sick of deceit.
Jane. Love, we've started the deception. We have to go on. If they find out now . . .
Trevor. That's right. If you hadn't invented *me*, you could just be two friends sharing a flat.
Sarah. Well, we've got to do something.
Jane. What?
Trevor. If you could just get rid of one set of parents, we could manage.

(Mrs Kempton *and* Mrs Lawrence *rise impatiently*)

Jane. How?
Trevor. Unless you'd rather get rid of me. I don't mind suicide in a good cause. I've often thought of it.

(Mrs Kempton *and* Mrs Lawrence *open their doors simultaneously*)

Mrs Kempton ⎫ (*together*) ⎧ Who was . . .
Mrs Lawrence ⎭ ⎨ Who was . . .
Mrs Kempton. I beg your pardon.
Mrs Lawrence. Not at all. (*To Sarah*) Who was it, dear?
Trevor. Wrong number. (*He looks from one to another*) Ah well, back to the kitchen. (*He returns to the kitchen and carries on making scones*)
Mrs Kempton (*as Trevor goes*) Why? (*She follows up a couple of stairs*)

SARAH (*quickly*) Oh, Mother, I don't think you know Jane's mother. Mrs Kempton, this is my mother.

MRS KEMPTON. How do you do?

MRS LAWRENCE. I'm so glad to meet you. (*Indicating with her right hand*) Sarah, why did Trevor . . . ?

JANE (*seizing her hand and pumping it*) And *we* haven't really been introduced, have we? I brought you some scones just now, but we never really met.

SARAH. Mother, this is Jane.

MRS LAWRENCE. How do you do? I was just telling my daughter, she never mentions you. Though apparently Trevor . . .

JANE. We lead rather separate lives, I'm afraid.

MRS KEMPTON. I'm sure Mrs Lawrence understands that, Jane.

MRS LAWRENCE. Sarah tells me your daughter's engaged to be married.

MRS KEMPTON (*looking towards the kitchen*) Yes, we . . .

SARAH (*jumping in almost hysterically*) And *Mr* Kempton, Mother. You haven't met Mr Kempton.

MRS KEMPTON. Trevor . . .

SARAH (*pulling Mr Lawrence over to the door* R *and waving through it*) Hullo, Mr Kempton! Hullo! This is my mother.

(MR KEMPTON *rises, bewildered*)

MR KEMPTON. What? What? (*sits again*)

SARAH (*to Mrs Kempton*) It's so nice to have met you. (*Pushing Mrs Lawrence back into her own room*) Come along, Mother. Mustn't let the scones get cold. (*She pushes Mrs Lawrence on the divan*)

MRS LAWRENCE (*astonished*) Will Trevor be long?

MRS KEMPTON (*coming downstairs*) Is that girl right in the head?

(SARAH *sits in the armchair down* R)

JANE (*moving down stage*) Of course she is.

MRS KEMPTON. There's no of course about it.

JANE. She's having—rather a difficult love affair at the moment. It makes her nervous.

MRS KEMPTON. What did that woman mean?

JANE. What woman?

MRS KEMPTON. "Will Trevor be long?"

JANE. Sarah's mother is not "that woman", Mother. Her name is Mrs Lawrence.

MRS KEMPTON. What did she mean: "Will Trevor be long?"

JANE. You must have misheard her.

MRS KEMPTON. Nonsense. I hope she understands that Trevor . . .

JANE. He advises her husband on scripts. It's a free-lance thing he does.

MRS KEMPTON. But she didn't know you. She had to be introduced to you.

JANE. She knows Trevor. I—(*inventing*)—I met Trevor through Sarah.

MRS KEMPTON. Indeed!

JANE. She gave a party, and of course she had to ask me. Trevor was one of the guests.

MRS KEMPTON. But you told me you met Trevor at the National Gallery, in front of a picture of small children being mobbed . . .

JANE (*bursting out*) Mother, for God's sake will you stop questioning everything I say?

MRS KEMPTON (*after a pause*) I don't know what's got into you today.

(MRS KEMPTON *goes back to Jane's room.* JANE *is left in the hall. She would like to join Sarah, looks at the door to that room, takes a step, but of course she cannot go in. At this point,* TREVOR, *in the kitchen, drops the mixing bowl and says, "Blast!"* JANE *hears him, is undecided whether to go up, but decides against, and follows her mother.* TREVOR *picks the bowl off the floor, and begins to dollop bits of the mixture on the tray*)

SARAH (*rising and moving down* R) I'm sorry. I really can't bear Jane's mother.

MRS LAWRENCE. But . . .

SARAH (*moving up* R) I don't want to talk about it. If you can't bear someone you can't.

MRS LAWRENCE. Where's Trevor?

SARAH. In the kitchen. Making . . . (*She breaks off*)

MRS LAWRENCE (*looking at the heap of scones*) Scones?

SARAH. I don't know what he's making.

MRS LAWRENCE. Harold, go and find out.

SARAH. No. Leave Trevor alone.

MRS LAWRENCE. Run along, Harold.

(MR LAWRENCE *rises*)

SARAH. Why?

MRS LAWRENCE. Because I want to talk to you privately, dear.

MR LAWRENCE (*after a pause, to Sarah*) Back soon. (*He goes to the hall, leaving the door open*)

SARAH. Father, you've forgotten your shoes.

MR LAWRENCE. Can't get them on. My feet have swollen.

(*The phone rings*)

SARAH. I'll go.

MRS LAWRENCE (*rising, calling*) Answer it, Harold, will you?

(MRS LAWRENCE *closes the door firmly and sits again.* MR LAWRENCE *answers the phone*)

MR LAWRENCE. Hullo? Hullo?

MRS KEMPTON. Harold dear, why don't you have a word with Trevor?

Mr Kempton. Eh?

Jane. What about?

Mr Lawrence. Hullo? Hullo?

Mrs Kempton. If you intend to marry Trevor, dear, then naturally your father ought to get to know him. In the kitchen, Harold.

Mr Kempton. Oh, all right.

Mr Lawrence. Speak up. What do you want? This is—(*looking*)
—one of those number things. Used to be Freemantle, but they
changed it.

Jane. Why does Father have to go. Trevor'll be back in a
moment.

Mrs Kempton. Because I want to have a little talk with you.

Jane. Why . . .

Mrs Kempton (*straight over her*) And I don't want your father to
be embarrassed.

Mr Lawrence. Hullo?

Mr Kempton (*rising, to Jane*) Back soon, Janie. (*He goes towards
the door*)

(Trevor *puts his wet dollop of mix in the oven*)

Jane. Father, you've forgotten your shoes.

Mr Kempton. Never mind. (*He closes the door behind him*)

Mr Lawrence. Hullo? (*He puts the phone down. To Mr Kempton*)
Nobody there.

Mr Kempton. Wrong number?

Mr Lawrence. Don't know. He didn't say.

Mr Kempton. How do you know there was anybody there at all.

Mr Lawrence. Asthma.

(Trevor, *wiping his hands on a tea-towel, starts to come downstairs.
He sees the two men and tries to escape but is too late*)

Mr Kempton (*moving to the foot of the stairs* L) There you are, young
man. I was just coming to have a word with you.

Mr Lawrence (*moving to the foot of the stairs* R) So was I.

Mr Kempton. Were you? Why?

Trevor (*coming down between them*) *Were* you? Ah, you were. Yes,
of course you were. You both were. But you won't both want to have
a word with me at the same time, will you? No, you won't.

Mr Kempton. My wife says we've got to get to know each other.

Mr Lawrence (*puzzled*) But you do know each other.

Trevor. Better. We should know each other better. We all
should. Everyone should.

Mr Lawrence. Trevor gives you advice.

Mr Kempton. No, that's what he gives you.

Mr Lawrence. He gives you advice about . . .

Trevor. I give everyone advice. It's a fault. Can't mind my own
business. Mr Kempton—Mr Lawrence. Mr Lawrence—Mr Kempton.

Mr Kempton ⎫
Mr Lawrence ⎬ (*together*) How do you do?

Trevor (*to Mr Kempton*) I expect you'd like to go to the loo, wouldn't you?

Mr Kempton. No, I wouldn't.

Trevor. Your wife went. It's nice in there.

Mr Kempton. No, I don't think so, thanks.

Mr Lawrence. Wait a minute. There's something I don't understand.

Trevor. Never miss an opportunity, because you don't know when you'll get another chance. Royalty do it. They're always doing it. And President de Gaulle and everybody.

Mr Kempton. No, thanks.

Trevor. You could be out walking. Any minute you'd pass a fountain. Or a mountain stream. Trickle, trickle! Imagine it.

Mr Kempton. I said, no, thank you.

Trevor. They've got blue bleach in the cistern. It colours the bowl when you flush. You pull the chain and the water goes zzzzzz.

Mr Lawrence. My wife wanted me to find out what you were doing in the kitchen.

Trevor. Making scones.

Mr Lawrence. Again? Bit obsessional, isn't it?

(*The phone rings*)

Mr Kempton (*to Trevor*) That for you?

Trevor. No. Why?

Mr Kempton. Thought it might be another of your . . .

Trevor. No. It isn't.

Mr Lawrence. Probably that fellow with asthma.

Trevor. The Chelsea Breather. (*To Mr Kempton*) It's someone who breathes.

Mr Kempton. I'll take it, then. (*He picks the phone up*) Hullo? . . . (*He listens then nods to the others*) Now look here, breather . . .

Mr Lawrence (*moving down* L *of Mr Kempton*) My wife says you've got to understand these people.

Mr Kempton. They need a shock. A sharp shock. (*Into the phone*) Breather, you need a shock.

Mr Lawrence. They did some experiments at the Howard League. Got a lot of them in a group, breathing at each other. Found they preferred that to using the phone.

Mr Kempton (*into the phone*) You run along and find some other breathers. We've had enough of you here. We . . . Hah! (*To the others*) Hung up. (*He puts the phone down*) We shan't hear from *him* again. What was that about scones? (*To Mr Lawrence*) He's always making scones, this fellow, but you never see any.

Mr Lawrence. Never *see* any?

(*The phone rings*)

Mr Kempton. I'll leave it off. (*He takes off the receiver*)

Trevor (*to Mr Kempton*) Look, sir, whatever you wanted to chat about, it's probably a bit personal, isn't it? So—(*indicating the L door*)—if Mr Lawrence wouldn't mind . . .

Mr Lawrence. Oh, I can't go back in there.

(*Smoke begins to emerge from the oven door*)

Trevor. Ah! (*He turns to Mr Kempton and indicates the R door*) Er . . .

Mr Kempton. Nor can I.

Trevor. Oh.

Mr Lawrence. My wife sent me out of the room. I can't go back.

Mr Kempton. So did mine. Wanted to have a heart-to-heart with Jane.

Mr Lawrence. Mine wanted to have a heart-to-heart with Sarah.

Trevor. What about? (*With quick second thoughts*) Wait! Don't tell me.

Mr Kempton. Can you smell anything burning?

(Trevor *sniffs, then hurries up to the kitchen.* Mr Kempton *follows, and* Mr Lawrence *follows him. The smoke is now thick.* Trevor *opens the oven door, looks inside, closes it again, then turns the oven off*)

Trevor. You have to watch them.

Mr Kempton. No scones, eh?

Mr Lawrence. You could have some of ours. We've got lots.

Trevor. There's some brandy in the cupboard.

Mr Kempton. Ah. Wonder which of the girls it belongs to.

Mr Lawrence. Sarah wouldn't mind.

Mr Kempton. Or Jane.

Trevor. Let's have some. (*He takes a bottle of brandy from a cupboard* R) Where do they keep the glasses?

Mr Kempton. If you don't know, who does? (*He goes to the cupboards*)

Trevor. How true! Of course, they're downstairs, aren't they in the—in Sarah's—Jane's . . .

Mr Lawrence. What? (*He starts for the door*)

Trevor. In the chiffonier.

Mr Kempton (*finding glasses in the kitchen cupboard*) Here you are.

(Mr Lawrence *returns and closes the door*)

Trevor. Oh, *those* glasses. (*Filling them*) You don't mind it neat. (*Toasting*) Cheers.

(*They all drink*)

I needed that.

Mr Kempton. Must be a bit of a strain. (*He moves* R *of the table*)

Trevor. You don't know how much.

Mr Lawrence. Meeting the parents. (*He moves* l *of the table*)

Trevor. Exactly. (*He moves above the table*)

Mr Kempton (*sitting*) Silly business. Unnecessary.

Trevor (*sitting*) Yes.

Mr Kempton (*sitting*) What young people do nowadays; it's nothing to do with their parents.

Trevor. No.

Mr Lawrence. You can't get Sarah's mother to see that, though.

Mr Kempton. Or Jane's.

Mr Lawrence. If two young people want to live together . . .

Mr Kempton. Oh, I don't know about living together.

Mr Lawrence (*to Trevor*) Anyway, you're not living together.

Mr Kempton. No, he's not.

Trevor. No, I'm not.

Mr Lawrence. But the point is, if you did want to, you'd do it. Please yourselves.

Mr Kempton (*to Trevor*) Would you?

Mr Lawrence. Your love life is your own affair. Nothing to do with your parents. (*To Mr Kempton*) Our generation should stay out of it.

Mr Kempton (*to Trevor*) But you're not going to live together?

Trevor. No, I'm not.

Mr Kempton. Jane's not that kind of girl. I'm sure she's not.

Trevor (*pouring more brandy in all three glasses*) Let's have another drink.

Mr Lawrence. Jane?

Mr Kempton. My daughter.

Mr Lawrence. Oh, Jane! Well, Jane would move out, I assume.

Mr Kempton. Why?

Mr Lawrence. Well, you weren't thinking . . .

Trevor. No, he wasn't.

Mr Kempton. What?

Trevor. You weren't thinking.

Mr Lawrence. No, I didn't imagine Jane would stay here if you were living together. Even my wife isn't that broad-minded.

Mr Kempton. She wouldn't want to stay here. No room, for one thing.

Mr Lawrence. Exactly.

Mr Kempton. I don't understand this. (*To Trevor*) You're not going to live together.

Mr Lawrence. I don't see why *you're* so bothered, Kempton.

Trevor. Cheers.

Mr Kempton }
Mr Lawrence } (*together*) Cheers.

Mr Lawrence. Funny.

Trevor. What is?

Mr Lawrence. My wife thought you might be queer.

Trevor. Queer?

Mr Lawrence. You know—homosexual. That kind of thing.

Mr Kempton. A nance. So did my wife.

Trevor. Oh, I don't think people say "nance" nowadays, do they?

Mr Lawrence. I told her everyone wears scent in ninety-sixty-seven.

Mr Kempton. I don't. Never have.

Trevor. Don't you?

Mr Kempton. I wouldn't mind, though. I like scent. I respond to it.

Trevor (shifting a little away uneasily) Do you?

Mr Lawrence. I've never been attracted to scent. Smell, yes. Not scent. Sweat. I've always found sweat attractive.

Trevor (wiping his hands nervously) Let me fill your glass. (He does so)

Mr Kempton. My wife wears Yardley's Lavender. It's not the same.

Mr Lawrence. My wife hardly sweats at all.

Mr Kempton. Funny my wife thought you were a nance.

Trevor. Hilarious.

Mr Kempton. Cheers.

(They all drink)

Mr Lawrence. Of course she used to sweat when she was younger. We went to Antibes for our honeymoon, and she sweated like a horse. Now she buys one of those roll-on deodorants.

(The conversational focus shifts downstairs. The men continue to drink in the kitchen)

Sarah (rising) This is ridiculous. I won't have this conversation.

Mrs Lawrence. He's not at all suitable.

Sarah (circling the divan) Suitability's got nothing to do with it. I'm not marrying him. You wanted me to be fulfilled. Well, I am fulfilled. Trevor fulfils me every Saturday afternoon, and now you're complaining.

Mrs Lawrence. A man like that couldn't fulfil anyone.

Sarah. What do you want? A blow-by-blow account?

Mrs Lawrence. Sarah!

Sarah. That shocks you, doesn't it. But you're supposed to be unshockable, Mother; you're the one that understands people. All my life you've told me to understand people, and now I'm understanding you.

Mrs Lawrence. What's that supposed to mean?

Sarah (moving down R) Try working it out. Why you've nagged at me to find a lover, and why you don't like it now I've found one.

Trevor. If your feet have swollen, you could put them in the fridge.

Mr Lawrence. Cheers.

TREVOR ⎱ (*together*) ⎰ Cheers.
MR KEMPTON ⎰ ⎱ Cheers.

MRS LAWRENCE (*rising to Sarah*) I don't want you to be unhappy.

(JANE, *in her own room, rises and moves down* L *below the armchair*)

SARAH. Don't you?

MRS KEMPTON (*rising to* R *of Jane*) I don't want you to be unhappy, Jane. A man like that . . .

JANE. Like what?

MRS KEMPTON. You know what I mean.

JANE. No. Tell me.

MRS KEMPTON. I don't say Trevor's—effeminate.

JANE. Then?

MRS KEMPTON. He's clearly unstable. He's not stable, dear. Not the sort of man you could rely on.

JANE. What if I'll settle for someone who'll rely on *me?*

MRS KEMPTON. Don't make debating points.

JANE. Damn you, Mother. I've had enough.

MRS KEMPTON. What?

SARAH. I've had enough.

JANE (*crossing below the table to* RC) You come here, meet some-one——

SARAH. —for the first time. (*Crossing below the table to* LC) You don't really know——

JANE. —a single bloody thing about him——

SARAH. —and in fifteen minutes——

JANE. —you've written him off.

SARAH. You tell me you're concerned about my future.

JANE. You don't give a damn for anyone but yourself.

SARAH. Just because Trevor wears scent——

JANE. —and bakes scones——

MRS KEMPTON. Jane! Please! (*She moves down* L *of the room*)

MRS LAWRENCE. Sarah! (*She moves down* R *of the room*)

SARAH (*turning up stage*) Oh, you're so broad-minded, Mother, so understanding . . .

JANE (*turning up stage*) Narrow-minded! Intolerant!

MRS LAWRENCE (*moving to Sarah*) But, Sarah, if you love him——

MRS KEMPTON (*moving to Jane*) —if you really love him that's a different matter. (*She sits on the divan*)

MRS LAWRENCE. If you're sure you love him. (*She sits on the divan*)

SARAH (*after a pause*) What? (*She sits* L *of Mrs Lawrence*)

JANE. Oh . . . (*She sits* R *of Mrs Kempton*)

MR KEMPTON. I'll tell my wife, "You've got it all wrong," I'll say.

MR LAWRENCE. Yes, *I'll* say that. (*To Trevor*) Don't you worry. I'll have a word with her.

MR KEMPTON. "He's not in the least queer. He's just a very obliging fellow."

Mr Lawrence. Cheers.

Mr Kempton ⎱ (*together*) ⎰ Cheers.
Trevor ⎰   ⎱ Cheers.

Jane. I'm sorry. I got carried away.

Sarah. I got carried away, Mother. I didn't mean to hurt you.

Mrs Lawrence. No, no, dear. I've no right to interfere.

Sarah. I was cruel. I didn't mean . . .

Mrs Lawrence. You did, dear.

Sarah. No.

Mrs Lawrence. And you were right. I look at myself, and what do I see? Prurient curiosity. And jealousy afterwards. I'm ashamed, Sarah.

Mrs Kempton. I've been a bossy woman all my life. Of course your father encourages it.

Jane. But, Mother . . .

Mrs Lawrence. Hearing you defend Trevor, "Lord, Lord," I thought, "I've had the impertinence to talk to this girl about fulfilment!"

Sarah. But I didn't mean to defend him. I just lost my temper.

Mrs Kempton. You wouldn't be my daughter if you didn't pick someone unsuitable to marry.

Jane. But, Mother, if he *is* unsuitable . . .

Mrs Lawrence. Your father used to be a very passionate man.

Mr Lawrence. I think she'd been reading the B.O. advertisements.

Mrs Lawrence. I forget who spoke to me about it.

Mr Lawrence. I couldn't very well tell her, "I *like* B.O."

Mr Kempton. Cheers.

Mr Lawrence ⎱ (*together*) ⎰ Cheers.
Trevor ⎰   ⎱ Cheers.

(*All the men drink*)

Jane. I'm trying to say, you may be right.

Sarah. I have had—doubts about Trevor.

Jane. If you really think I should give him up . . .

Mrs Kempton. No, dear, no.

Mrs Lawrence. No, Sarah. It's your own life.

Sarah. Perhaps if I didn't see him for a while . . .

Jane. If we tried a separation until I feel clearer in my mind.

Sarah. I could talk to him. If he really loves me——

Jane. —he'd want me to be certain of what I feel; I'm sure of that.

Mrs Lawrence. Perhaps later . . .

Sarah. No, I'll do it now.

Mrs Lawrence. He's still in the kitchen with your father.

Mrs Kempton. Your father's talking to him in the kitchen.

Jane. Yes, that's right. (*Rising and moving to the door*) I'll send Daddy down.

SARAH (*rising and moving to the door*) I shan't be long. I think it's better if he leaves straight away.
MRS LAWRENCE (*rising to Sarah*) Oh, my dear, if you're sure.
SARAH. I am.

(MRS LAWRENCE *kisses Sarah*)

JANE. I shan't bring Trevor back. He's bound to be a bit upset.
MRS KEMPTON (*rising to Jane*) My brave girl! (*She kisses Jane*)

(SARAH *and* JANE *go into the hall, closing the doors behind them.* MRS LAWRENCE *and* MRS KEMPTON *sigh, exhausted, move to their divans, and sit*)

MR LAWRENCE. Cheers.
MR KEMPTON. Cheers.
TREVOR (*rising*) Excuse me. (*He moves slowly to the kitchen door*)
JANE. I've promised to give him up.
SARAH. So have I.
JANE. I said I'd talk to him, and he'd leave right away.
SARAH. Have you got the five pounds?
JANE. In my bag.
SARAH. Oh, love! Love!

(JANE *and* SARAH *kiss.* TREVOR *comes downstairs*)

JANE. Trevor . . .
TREVOR. I don't feel well.
SARAH. No!
TREVOR. I had a lot of beer in the pub. And then vodka. And I've been drinking brandy with your fathers. I feel very strange.
JANE. Get him into the bathroom.

(JANE *and* SARAH *take* TREVOR *to the bathroom*)

You'll be all right, Trevor. You'll be all right.
TREVOR (*last words*) I'm not Trevor.

(JANE, SARAH *and* TREVOR *exit into the bathroom*)

MR LAWRENCE (*sipping brandy*) Think he's all right?
MR KEMPTON (*sipping brandy*) My wife doesn't care for him.
MR LAWRENCE. Looked a bit shaky, I thought.
MR KEMPTON. Oh—that. Probably not used to it.
MR LAWRENCE. Used to what?
MR KEMPTON. Drinking brandy in the afternoon. Got out of the habit.

(*The door to downstairs is opened with a latch-key.* MR HUDSON *enters. He looks round, sees the phone is off the hook and replaces it censoriously. He looks about him, then crouches to peer through the keyhole of the door* R)

Tell you a devil for the brandy. Old Johnny Chinaman.

Mr Lawrence. Johnny?

Mr Kempton. Manner of speaking. Old Johnny Chink.

Mr Lawrence. Ah!

Mr Kempton. Used to see a lot of those fellows during the war. Chiang Kai-shek's fellows. Devils for brandy. They'd knock it back by the tumblerfull. "Banzai," they'd say . . .

(Mr Hudson *peeps through the keyhole of the door* l)

Mr Lawrence (*pouring*) Couldn't have been "Banzai".

Mr Kempton. By George, you're right there. What *did* they say. I wonder? Neat brandy. Tigers for it. (*Raising his glass*) Banzai.

Mr Lawrence. Cheers.

Mr Kempton. No, no, old boy. It was something Chinese. Something colloquial. You'd learn it off a record nowadays, but in my time we actually had to meet these fellows.

(Mr Hudson *is puzzled by what he's seen through the keyhole of the doors. He starts to go upstairs to the kitchen. There is a gurgle from* Trevor *in the bathroom*)

Jane (*off*) Get his head under water.

(Mr Hudson *goes to the bathroom door and peers through*)

Mr Lawrence. I suppose he's all right. Trevor.

Mr Kempton (*rising and moving to the kitchen door*) I'll go and see. I could do with a leak. Too much talk about fountains.

(Mr Kempton *descends the stairs and sees Mr Hudson*)

Ah. Bit of queue, is there?

Mr Hudson (*startled*) What?

Mr Kempton. Bit of a queue. (*He notices the phone*) That's funny. Thought I left it off. (*He takes it off again*) I hope he won't be long in there. At my age, the old kidneys . . .

Mr Hudson. You shouldn't leave the telephone off the hook.

Mr Kempton. Why not?

Mr Hudson (*replacing it*) The Post Office don't like it.

Mr Kempton. You're from the Post Office, are you?

Mr Hudson. Er . . .

Mr Kempton. Thought I hadn't seen you before. (*Moving towards the bathroom*) Tell you what; let's bang on the door. He might have passed out. (*He knocks on the bathroom door*)

Mr Hudson (*following Mr Kempton up stage*) Who?

Mr Kempton. I had to climb over a lavatory door once in Dehra Dun. Been knocking it back a bit with a friend of mine. Brother officer, you know. In he went, locked the door, never came out. Couldn't let him down, so over the top I went. It was pretty to see him lying there, curled around the bowl.

Mr Hudson. *Who* may have passed out?

MR KEMPTON. But it was rather difficult to explain to the brigadier, when we both came out together.

MR HUDSON. *Who* . . .

(MRS KEMPTON *rises and moves to the door*)

MR KEMPTON. You wouldn't know him. Lumley—Mahratha Light Infantry. Oh—in there? My daughter's fiancé.

(MRS KEMPTON *enters the hall*)

MRS KEMPTON. Harold, to whom are you talking?

MR KEMPTON. Fellow from the Post Office come in for a bit of a leak.

MRS KEMPTON. From the *Post Office!* In here?

MR KEMPTON (*to Mr Hudson*) By George, that's true. Just because you're in the government service, that doesn't give you the right to barge into a private flat every time you want to . . .

MR HUDSON. I am not . . .

MR KEMPTON. Bloody Trades Unions throwing their weight around again. Dammit, you've got pillar-boxes for that sort of thing.

MRS KEMPTON. Why should a man from the Post Office . . .

MR KEMPTON. I'd left the phone off the hook. (*To Mr Hudson*) Had to. One of those breathers kept ringing up. Dring! Dring! Couldn't hear yourself speak. He'll ring again in a minute.

(MRS LAWRENCE *rises and moves to the door*)

MR HUDSON. No, he won't.

MRS KEMPTON. How did he get in?

(MRS LAWRENCE *looks into the hall*)

MRS LAWRENCE. Harold!

MR KEMPTON. Yes? (*Turning to her*) How do you do? I'm Jane's father; I don't think we've met. And this is a man from the Post Office come in for a . . .

MRS KEMPTON. That will do, Harold.

MR KEMPTON (*going on into Sarah's room*) You don't mind if I sit down? Not much point in standing around when you're not even first in the queue. (*He sits in the armchair down* R *and crosses his legs*)

MRS LAWRENCE (*from the doorway*) I was calling my husband.

MR KEMPTON. Ah! (*Calling over his shoulder*) Lawrence, your wife wants you.

(MR LAWRENCE *hears the call and stands*)

MR LAWRENCE. What? (*He finishes his drink*)

MRS KEMPTON (*to Mrs Lawrence*) I have been trying to discover how this man gained entry to the flat. (*To Mr Hudson*) If you're from the Post Office, why aren't you in uniform?

MR HUDSON. I'm not from the Post Office.

MRS LAWRENCE. A burglar? (*To Mrs Kempton*) Is he a burglar?
MR HUDSON. I'm the landlord.
MR KEMPTON (*rising*) I say! (*He takes a scone and moves down* L) Lots of scones here! (*He sits* L)
MR HUDSON. I came to put the phone back on the hook.

(MR LAWRENCE *descends the stairs*)

MRS LAWRENCE. Harold, where is Trevor?
MR LAWRENCE. Kempton went to find out. (*Passing Mr Hudson*) How do you do? (*He sees Mr Kempton through the open door*) Kempton, where's Trevor?
MR KEMPTON. Still in there. Probably passed out.
MR LAWRENCE (*entering the room* L) You've found the scones, I see.
MR KEMPTON. Have one.
MR LAWRENCE. Not allowed. Tea? (*He sits in the armchair* R)
MR KEMPTON. God, no.
MR LAWRENCE. Ah! You haven't . . . ?
MR KEMPTON. Not yet. I told you. He's still in there.
MRS LAWRENCE (*stepping into the room* L) Harold, this man says he's the landlord.
MR KEMPTON. How did he get in, then?
MRS LAWRENCE (*to Mr Hudson*) How did you . . .

(MR HUDSON *crosses below Mrs Lawrence into the room* L *and moves* C)

MR HUDSON (*to Mr Kempton; indignantly*) I have a key. I let myself in. I have the right to do so. (*He looks round*) And now I shall go.

(MRS KEMPTON *joins Mrs Lawrence in the doorway, barring Mr Hudson's way back to the hall*)

MRS KEMPTON. There's no proof of that.
MRS KEMPTON (*rising*) That's right. He could be a damned thief, come sneaking in here, pretending he wants to use the loo. Come here, sneak thief; I'm going to search your pockets.
MRS LAWRENCE. He said he wanted to put the phone back on the hook.
MR KEMPTON. How did he know the phone was off the hook?

(*There is a pause.* MR HUDSON *is now uneasy.* MRS LAWRENCE *and* MRS KEMPTON *come into the room, so that he is surrounded*)

MRS KEMPTON. Well, my man?
MRS LAWRENCE. How did you know the phone was . . .
MR LAWRENCE. It *was* off, though.
MR KEMPTON. What?
MR LAWRENCE. I mean, he is right. The phone was off the hook.
MRS LAWRENCE. But how could he know that?
MR HUDSON (*after a pause*) I have—ways of knowing.
MR LAWRENCE. What ways?

F

Mr Hudson. Mind your own business.

Mr Kempton (*after a pause*) By George, you're not the landlord at all; you're that breather. You've been ringing up and breathing at us, and when I took the phone off the hook . . .

Mr Hudson. I'm the landlord. I have a key. It's natural for me to be here.

Mr Kempton. You stole them, you breather.

Mr Hudson. No.

Mr Lawrence. I suppose he could be both.

Mrs Lawrence. What, Harold?

Mr Lawrence. Landlord and breather. He could be both.

(Mrs Kempton *closes the door of the room*)

Mrs Kempton (*bearing down on Mr Hudson*) Do you mean that a man who breathes at women on the telephone has the keys to my daughter's flat?

(Trevor, Sarah *and* Jane *come into the hall cautiously. The girls help Trevor on with his coat*)

Sarah. It's all right. There's nobody here.

Mr Hudson. But I never use it.

Trevor. Shouldn't I say good-bye to *anyone?*

Jane. No.

Mrs Kempton. Never use it? Of course you use it. You're using it now.

Jane. Just go. Quietly. We'll explain.

Trevor. It's so impolite. Both of me just creeping off like this.

Mr Hudson. Only because the telephone was off the hook.

Sarah. Good-bye, Trevor.

Jane. Good-bye, Trevor.

Trevor. Wait a sec. I forgot something. (*He returns to the bathroom*)

Mr Hudson. You can ask your daughters. I never come here.

(Trevor *flushes the W.C.*)

Mr Kempton. By George, he's out. (*He goes quickly to the door*) Excuse me.

Hudson. But . . .

Mr Kempton. No, old boy. You've forfeited your turn. (*He goes into the hall*) Jane, there's a breather in here, says he's your landlord (*Passing Trevor*) There you are, Trevor. Feeling better?

Trevor. Much better.

Mr Kempton. You took your time.

Trevor. Sorry.

(Mr Kempton *exits to the bathroom, closing the door*)

Sarah. Trevor! Go!

Mrs Kempton. Jane, are you there?

Mrs Lawrence (*moving to the door*) Sarah dear, just come in for a moment, will you please? Oh, is Trevor going? I'll just have a word with him.

Sarah. Mother, I've already had a word with him.

(Sarah *moves towards her mother.* Jane *and* Trevor *moves nearer to the front door*)

Trevor. Yes, she has, and I quite understand. Good-bye, Mrs Lawrence. Good-bye, Sarah. Good-bye, Jane. (*He opens the front door*)

Mrs Kempton (*moving to the door*) Is that Trevor?

Mrs Lawrence. He's just leaving.

Trevor (*calling*) Good-bye, Mrs Kempton.

Mrs Kempton (*entering the hall*) I'll have a word with him before he goes. (*To Jane*) Go on in, Jane dear, I just want a word with Trevor.

Mrs Lawrence. Run along, Sarah.

Sarah. Mother, *you* don't want a word with him.

Mrs Lawrence. Just to show there are no hard feelings, dear.

(Jane *and* Sarah *look at each other, and at Trevor. Then they go into Sarah's room.* Mr Hudson *regards them piteously*)

Mr Hudson. There's been a mistake.

(Jane *sits on the divan*)

Sarah (*moving up* R) Yes.

(Mr Hudson *moves up* L. Mrs Kempton *closes the door and moves* L *of Trevor*)

Mrs Kempton. Now, Trevor . . .

Trevor. Please, please! I know what you both want to say.

Mrs Lawrence. All *I* wanted to tell you . . .

Trevor. No need to put it into words.

Mrs Kempton. There are no hard feelings.

Trevor. Just say good-bye. Believe me, I do understand. It's better.

Mrs Lawrence (*to Mrs Kempton*) No hard feelings?

Mrs Kempton. None.

Mrs Lawrence. But I have no hard feelings for Trevor. I'm the one with no hard feelings.

Mrs Kempton. Why should *you* have no hard feelings?

Trevor. Surely if neither of you has no hard feelings, there's no need to go on about it.

Mrs Lawrence. Because Sarah is going to give him up.

Mrs Kempton. No, no, my dear, Jane is going to give him up.

Mr Lawrence. Sarah's going to give the affair time to cool.

Mrs Kempton. Jane wants to be certain what she feels for him.

Trevor. Mrs Lawrence . . .

Mrs Kempton. Trevor is Jane's fiancé, Mrs Lawrence.

TREVOR. Mrs Kempton . . .

MRS LAWRENCE. Trevor is Sarah's lover, Mrs Kempton.

TREVOR (*after a pause*) Anyway, if they're both going to give me up there's no harm done, is there?

(*The W.C. is flushed.* MR KEMPTON *comes out of the bathroom to between Trevor and Mrs Lawrence*)

MRS KEMPTON. Harold, take Trevor into Miss Lawrence's room.

MR KEMPTON. *Take* him?

(TREVOR *looks from Mr Kempton to the women, then closes the door*)

TREVOR. I'll come quietly. (*He goes into Sarah's room*)

(MR KEMPTON *follows Trevor*)

SARAH. They know?

TREVOR. Yes. (*He sits* C *on the divan*)

MR LAWRENCE. Hello, Trevor. We've caught your breather.

MR HUDSON. I do not breathe. I have a right to telephone my own tenants.

MR KEMPTON (*moving down* L) I don't understand this. (*He sits on the armchair down* L)

(MRS LAWRENCE *and* MRS KEMPTON *go into Sarah's room.* MRS KEMPTON *sits* R *on the divan.* MRS LAWRENCE *closes the door and stands by it*)

MRS KEMPTON. Now.

MR HUDSON. I am not obliged to explain to you. All my tenants are single women. I have a duty . . .

MRS KEMPTON. What is this person talking about.

MR HUDSON. I do not breathe at women.

MRS LAWRENCE. No time for that now. Well, Sarah?

MRS KEMPTON. Well, Jane?

MR LAWRENCE. What's up?

MR KEMPTON. Don't ask me.

SARAH. Mother's found out that Trevor's Jane's fiancé as well as my lover.

MR LAWRENCE. What?

MR KEMPTON. Steady on.

SARAH. He's single as well as married, and he works for the B.B.C. as well as Shell.

TREVOR. I.C.I.

MRS KEMPTON. Mr Hudson . . .

MR HUDSON. My name's Hudson.

TREVOR. Not Trevor?

MR HUDSON. Wallace.

MRS KEMPTON. I'm waiting for an explanation.

JANE. We put him up to it.

MRS LAWRENCE (*moving up stage*) Why?

JANE. You wanted Sarah to have a lover. (*To Mrs Kempton*) You wanted me to be engaged. You both went on about it. We invented Trevor. Both of him. Then you wanted to meet him. Well, you only come up to London one day a year; it didn't seem too difficult. We couldn't know Sarah's parents would arrive on the same day.

MRS KEMPTON. But why?

MR HUDSON. You've moved the furniture. That wardrobe belongs in the bedroom.

MR LAWRENCE. I thought you said you never used your key.

MRS KEMPTON. The bedroom?

SARAH. We don't have two bed-sitters. We have a bedroom and a living-room. The two couches push together.

TREVOR. Sarah, love, enough's enough.

SARAH. No, I'm sick of it. I'm sick of deception.

JANE. Sarah!

SARAH. I told you, I'm sick of deception. (*To Mrs Lawrence*) Jane and I live together, Mother.

MRS LAWRENCE. Yes, dear. You share a flat.

SARAH. We *live* together. There isn't any Trevor. There's just Jane and me.

MRS KEMPTON. Yes, my dear; you told us. It was a stupid deception, but I'm sure your mother won't hold it against you.

SARAH. Jane, *tell* them.

JANE. Sarah means . . .

MRS KEMPTON. We know what she means, dear. You and Sarah share a flat.

SARAH. Yes.

MRS KEMPTON. Naturally you're friends . . .

SARAH. Yes, we are friends.

MRS KEMPTON (*rising on*) It would be very inconvenient if you weren't. And since you're both a little shy—(*to Mrs Lawrence*)—Jane's always been shy . . .

MRS LAWRENCE. And Sarah. Ridiculous. Pathologically.

MRS KEMPTON. Naturally you're embarrassed that you've neither of you found a young man yet.

SARAH. Yet!

MRS KEMPTON. I blame myself. (*To Mrs Lawrence*) I push Jane too much; I know I do. I had to push her when she was a girl, or she'd never have done anything.

MRS LAWRENCE. They're a more puritanical generation now. We were very frank about sex in the thirties. Perhaps I'm too outspoken. I brought Sarah up on D. H. Lawrence.

MRS KEMPTON. Did you!

(MR KEMPTON *tries to get Mr Lawrence's shoes on*)

MRS LAWRENCE. So she invents a lover. Then she's ashamed.

MRS KEMPTON (*to Jane*) You chose to play a joke on us, my dear. Not in very good taste, but perhaps we deserved it.

SARAH. Daddy—Mr Kempton—do you believe this?
MR KEMPTON (*fiddling with the shoes*) I can't get these shoes on.
MRS LAWRENCE. They're mine.
MR KEMPTON. Oh, is that it?

(MR LAWRENCE *and* MR KEMPTON *changes places*)

MRS KEMPTON. I don't know whose particular friend Trevor happens to be.
SARAH. Nobody's. I picked him up in a pub.
MRS LAWRENCE. There! You do go out and meet people.
SARAH. We never go out.
MRS KEMPTON. Anyway, now you have met Trevor, I'm sure you'll get to know each other better.
TREVOR. My name's not Trevor.
MRS LAWRENCE. You must bring him down to Bury St Edmunds, Sarah.
MRS KEMPTON. Jane, you must bring him to Torquay. (*To Mr Kempton*) Harold!

(MR KEMPTON *gets up*)

SARAH (*sitting* R *on the divan, to Jane*) They're going. They won't listen.

(JANE *goes slowly to Mr Kempton down* R)

MR KEMPTON (*kisses Jane awkwardly*) 'Bye, Janey. Er . . .
JANE. Yes?

(MR KEMPTON *looks at his wife, then decides against what he was going to say.* MR LAWRENCE *puts on his shoes*)

MR KEMPTON. I'll just get my shoes. (*He goes into Jane's room and puts them on*)
MRS KEMPTON. Will you get your father's coat, Jane?
SARAH. You don't want to know, then?
MRS KEMPTON (*moving to the door*) Good-bye, Sarah my dear. I'm so glad to have met you at last. (*To Mrs Lawrence*) Good-bye, Mrs Lawrence. (*To Mr Lawrence*) Good-bye.

(MRS KEMPTON *and* JANE *go out into the hall and* JANE *gets the coats.* MR KEMPTON *joins them.* MRS LAWRENCE *moves down* R)

SARAH. Mother, you've been open-minded all your life. You've boasted of it. Your mind was always so open, I used to fall in.
JANE. Here's your coat.

(MRS KEMPTON *kisses her.* JANE *is entirely unresponding*)

MRS KEMPTON. Good-bye, my dear. You know we always enjoy seeing you.
MR KEMPTON. 'Bye, Janey. (*He kisses her as he takes her coat*)
JANE. Good-bye, Daddy.

(Mrs Kempton *opens the front door.* Mr Kempton *exits.* Mrs Lawrence *sits in the armchair down* R)

Mrs Kempton. You're such a silent sulky little thing when you're upset.

(Mrs Kempton *exits*)

Jane. Good-bye, Mother. (*She remains, gazing after them, then closes the door*)

Sarah. I was cruel to you just now, do you remember, when we were arguing about Trevor? I was nervous and hating everything and I lost my temper. I mocked you for being unshockable, and always understanding people.

(Jane *comes to the door of the room* L)

I said you ought to understand yourself for a start. And you took it, Mother. You shamed me by seeing what I saw, and accepting it. Now accept me.

Mrs Lawrence. You overdramatize, dear. (*To Jane*) Doesn't she overdramatize, Jane?

Sarah (*rising and moving to Mrs Lawrence*) Do you remember that Easter I didn't come home? Jane didn't go home either. We'd just met—picked each other up in the National Gallery.

Mrs Lawrence. You met in the National Gallery?

Trevor. In front of a picture of small children being mobbed by apes.

(Jane *sits on the upstage* R *corner of the divan*)

Sarah. We went away together that Easter, to a cottage near Long Melford. It was down a long muddy path. We took Jane's haversack, full of healthfood bread and salami and tins of stuffed vine leaves and a pheasant in jelly, and we bought eggs and cream from the farm. We'd lie in bed very late, and one of us would wash up while the other chopped wood for the fire, and we'd go for long walks in the afternoons. It was warm spring weather. We walked through wild anemones and celandines, through primroses and blue-bells and wild garlic. We hunted for fossils in the quarry. At night, we'd pile the fire high with wood, and sit in front of it, playing bezique and eating chocolates.

Mrs Lawrence (*rising*) We must get our coats. (*She moves to the door*)

Sarah (*following Mrs Lawrence*) I'm trying to explain something to you, Mother. I'm trying to get you to feel something.

Mrs Lawrence. Sarah dear, you don't need to explain to me about friendship. It's very rare. (*To Jane*) Real friends are very rare, and much to be prized. (*To Mr Lawrence*) Harold!

Mr Lawrence (*rising*) Off now, are we?

SARAH. I wasn't talking about friendship, Mother. I was talking about love. We made love.

MRS LAWRENCE (*ignoring this*) Good-bye, Jane. I'm so happy to have met you. (*She goes into the hall*) Good-bye, Trevor. (*She picks up Mr Lawrence's coat and her own*)

MR LAWRENCE (*following*) 'Bye, Trevor—Jane . . . (*He kisses Sarah*)

TREVOR. Good-bye.

(SARAH *follows her parents into the hall*)

MRS LAWRENCE (*giving Mr Lawrence his coat*) If you do want to bring Trevor down for a week-end, dear, we've plenty of room.

SARAH. Mother, if you're going to understand people, you'd better begin with what they do in bed.

MRS LAWRENCE (*going*) Sarah, Sarah, *how* you exaggerate!

MR LAWRENCE (*going*) I like Trevor, you know. And your mother's quite come round to him.

(MR *and* MRS LAWRENCE *exit.* SARAH *follows them to the door*)

SARAH. Oh . . .

(SARAH *slams the door, then slowly moves down the hall and enters her room*)

TREVOR. What did you expect?

(SARAH *sits in the armchair down* R)

JANE. Shut up, Trevor.

MR HUDSON. If I understand you . . . (*He goes to the door and closes it*)

JANE. Yes? (*She rises*)

MR HUDSON. There will be no question of—young men.

JANE (*moving slowly down* LC) What?

MR HUDSON. In the flat. Visiting. (*He looks at Trevor*) Well, they may visit. From time to time. But . . .

JANE. We have few visitors, and no young men. You understand correctly.

MR HUDSON. Ah! I let all my properties to single women, you see. I like to feel—in a fatherly relationship. One can do very little to discourage young men, but I dislike them visiting.

TREVOR. What *can* you do?

MR HUDSON. If there are too many, I don't renew the lease.

JANE. We shall be model tenants in that respect.

MR HUDSON. Thank you. You won't object if I—ring up from time to time? I shan't speak, of course.

JANE. We'll know who it is.

MR HUDSON. I'll say farewell then. Miss Kempton—Miss Lawrence—Mr . . .

TREVOR. Good-bye. (*He goes and opens the door for Mr Hudson*)

MR HUDSON (*going down the hall*) I'll show myself out.

TREVOR. You know your way.

(MR HUDSON *exits*)

(*After a pause*) It's just us then. (*He moves down* L *and sits*) Not my most successful performance, I'm afraid.

JANE (*moving* C) It wasn't your fault.

TREVOR. They do know, you know.

JANE. Yes.

TREVOR. It's just that they don't want to put it into words.

JANE. No.

TREVOR. You can't blame them.

JANE. I don't.

TREVOR. Sarah does.

JANE. Yes.

TREVOR (*after a pause*) I don't suppose you'll be taking me down to Bury St Edmunds. Or Torquay.

JANE. No.

TREVOR. Thank you for the five pounds.

JANE. You earned it.

TREVOR. No, really, I enjoyed—(*he rises*)—well, I did enjoy it actually. (*He moves slowly to the door*) Shall I see you around? (*He opens the door and pauses*) If you were going out for a drink or anything. I'm often in that pub when I'm not working.

SARAH. We don't go out, Trevor. We hardly ever go out.

TREVOR (*after a pause*) My name's not Trevor.

TREVOR *goes along the hall and exits,* JANE *and* SARAH *listen until the front door closes.* JANE *sits on the arm of Sarah's chair and puts a hand round her shoulders. The lights fade, leaving a single box of hard, white light; then all front lights fade, leaving the two girls back-lit. They sit very still. There is a pause, then—*

the CURTAIN *falls*

FURNITURE AND PROPERTY LIST

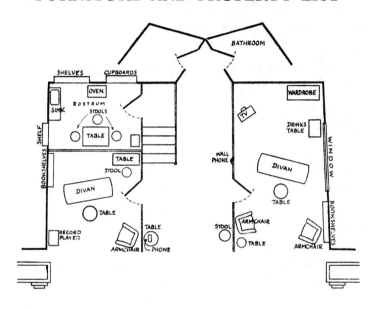

On stage: ROOM DOWN R:

Bookshelves (R) *In them:* books

Dressing-table (up L) *On it:* make-up, mirror

Stool

Divan. *On it:* book

Coffee-table (below divan) *On it:* tray with 4 cups and saucers, plates, knives, forks, teaspoons, jam, butter, cake

Armchair

Record player

Fitted carpet

KITCHEN UP R:

Sink unit (R) *On it:* kettle

Towel rail. *On it:* 2 towels

Cooker (up C) *In it:* 2 batches of cooked scones, smoke box

Refrigerator. *In it:* milk, eggs

Shelves and cupboards. *On or in them:* scone basket, napkins, plates, cups, saucers, knives, teaspoons, teapot, milk jug, pot plant on plate, jam, butter, tray, bottle of brandy, glasses, flour, baking tray, oven mitt, packet of Scone Mix

Table (down c) *On it:* scone dough, scone cutter, flour sifter, rolling-pin, plastic mixing bowl, baking tray
3 stools
On hook behind door: apron
Window curtains

HALL:
Telephone on table (down R)
Wall telephone (L)
Stool (down L)
On wall L: hooks
Fitted carpet

ROOM L:
Wardrobe (up L)
Small chair (up L)
2 armchairs (down R and L)
Divan
Drinks table (L) *On it:* vodka, tonic water, glasses, ashtray
Bookshelves (L) *In them:* books
Coffee-table
Occasional table (down R) *On it:* cigarette-box, lighter, ashtray
Television set, with closed doors (up R)
Fitted carpet

Personal: JANE: cigarette, watch
SARAH: latchkey
MR LAWRENCE: cigars, matches
TREVOR: notebook, pencil
MR HUDSON: latchkey

FURNITURE AND LIGHTING PLOT

Property fittings required: nil
A composite setting
THE APPARENT SOURCES OF LIGHT are windows in the "fourth wall"

THE MAIN ACTING AREAS are up RC, down RC, up and down C, LC, down L

To open: Effect of February afternoon light. *N.B.* Lighting should be in extreme contrast to that of "The Coffee Lace", sharp and precise

Cue 1   SARAH: "I'm sick of deception"   (Page 79)
General lighting becomes gradually colder

Cue 2   JANE puts her arm round Sarah   (Page 83)
Fade to a single spot, then to back lighting on the two girls

EFFECTS PLOT

PRINTED AND BOUND IN GREAT BRITAIN BY
BUTLER & TANNER LTD.,
FROME AND LONDON